THE WAY INTO THE HOLIEST
BY

F.B. Meyer

FOREWORD

F.B. Meyer (1847-1929) was a Baptist pastor in England as well as an author on many religious books and sermons. Meyer, a friend of D.L. Moody, was often described as The Archbishop of Free Churches.

The Way Into the Holiest

PREFACE

This Epistle bears no name of author, or designation of church. But it needs neither. In every sentence we can detect the Authorship of the Holy Spirit, and feel that it has a message, not to one age, but to all ages, not to one community, but to the universal Church.

We do not therefore discuss questions which are amply treated in every commentary, but set ourselves at once to derive those great spiritual lessons which are enshrined in these sublime words.

And probably there is no better way of vindicating the authority of the Pentateuch than by showing that it lay at the basis of the teaching of the early Church, and that the Book of Leviticus especially was the seed-plot of New Testament Theology.

There are two strong tendencies flowing around us in the present day: the one, to minimise the substitutionary aspect of the death of Christ; the other, to exaggerate the importance of mere outward rite. To each of these the study of this great Epistle is corrective.

We are taught that our Lord's death was a Sacrifice. We are taught also that we have passed from the realm of shadows into that of realities.

These chapters are altogether inadequate for the treatment of so vast a theme, but such as they are, they are sent forth, in dependence on the Divine Blessing, in the fervent hope that they may serve to make more clear and plain to those who would find and enter it, the Way into the Holiest of all.

CHAPTER 1: THE WORD OF GOD

GOD, Who at sundry times and in divers manners spoke in time past to the fathers by the prophets, has in these last days spoken to us by His Son." (Hebrews 1.1-2).

What word could more fittingly stand at the head of the first line of the first paragraph in this noble epistle! Each structure must rest on Him as foundation, each tree must spring from Him as root; each design and enterprise must originate in Him as source.

"IN THE BEGINNING - GOD," is a worthy motto to inscribe at the commencement of every treatise, be it the ponderous volume or the ephemeral tract. And with that name we commence our attempt to gather up some of the glowing lessons which were first addressed to the persecuted and wavering Hebrews in the primitive age, but have ever been most highly prized by believing Gentiles throughout the universal Church.

The feast was originally spread for the children of the race of Abraham; but who shall challenge our right to the crumbs?

In the original Greek, the word "God" is preceded by two other words which describe the variety and multiplicity of His revelation to man. And the whole verse is full of interest as detailing the origin and authority of the Word of God, and as illustrating the great law which appears in so many parts of the works of God, and has been fitly called the law of variety in unity.

That law operates in Nature, the earliest book of God. No thoughtful man can look around him without being arrested by the infinite variety that meets him on every side. "All flesh is not the same flesh; . . . there are celestial bodies, and bodies terrestrial: but the glory of the celestial is one; and the glory of the terrestrial is another. . . . One star differs from another star in glory."

You cannot match two faces in a crowd; two leaves in a forest; or two flowers in the woodlands of spring. It would seem as if the moulds in which natural products are being shaped are broken up and cast aside as soon as one result has been attained. And it is this which affords such an infinite field for investigation and enjoyment, forbidding all fear of monotony or weariness of soul.

And yet, amid all natural variety, there is a marvellous unity. Every part of the universe interlocks by subtle and delicate links with every other part. You cannot disturb the balance anywhere without sending a shock of disturbance through the whole system. Just as in some majestic Gothic minster the same idea repeats itself in bolder or slighter forms, so do the same great thoughts recur in tree and flower, in molecule and planet, in tiny atom and man. And all this because, if you penetrate to Nature's heart, you meet God.

"Of Him, and through Him, and to Him, are all things." (Romans 11.36). "There are diversities of operations, but it is the same God Who works all in all." (1 Corinthians 12.6). The unity that pervades Nature's temple is the result of its having originated from one mind, and having been effected by one hand, the mind and hand of God.

That law also operates throughout the Scriptures. There is as great variety there as in Nature. They were written in different ages. Some in the days of "the fathers"; others at "the end of these days" for us.

In the opening chapters, under the guidance of the Spirit of God, Moses has embodied fragments of hallowed tradition, which passed from lip to lip in the tents of the patriarchs; and its later chapters were written when the holy city, Jerusalem, had already been smitten to the ground by the mailed hand of Titus.

They were written in different countries. These in the deserts of Arabia, those under the shadow of the pyramids, and others amid the tides of life that swept through the greatest cities of Greece and Rome.

You can detect in some the simple pastoral life of Palestine, in others the magnificence of Nebuchadnezzar's empire. In one there is the murmur of the blue Aegean; and in several the clank of the fetters in the Roman prison cell.

They were written by men belonging to various ranks, occupations, and methods of thought. Shepherds and fishermen, warriors and kings, the psalmist, the prophet, and the priest; some employing the stately religious Hebrew, others the Aramaic patois, others the polished Greek.

There is every variety of style, from the friendly letter, or sententious proverb, to the national history, or the carefully prepared treatise, in which thought and expression glow as in the fires -- but all contributing their quota to the symmetry and beauty of the whole.

And yet, throughout the Bible, there is an indubitable unity. What else could have led mankind to look upon these sixty-six books as being so unmistakably related to each other that they must be bound up together under a common cover?

There has been something so unique in these books that they have always stood and fallen together. To disintegrate one has been to loose them all. Belief in one has led to belief in all. Their hands are linked and locked so tightly that where one goes all must follow.

And though wise and clever men have tried their best, they have never been able to produce a single treatise containing that undefinable quality which gives these their mysterious oneness; and to lack which is fatal to the claims of any book to be included with them, or to demand the special veneration and homage of mankind.

The world is full of religious books, but the man who has fed his religious life on the Bible will tell in a moment the difference between them and the Scriptures of the Old and New Testaments.

The eye can instantly detect the absence of life in the artificial flower, the tongue can immediately and certainly detect the absence or presence of a certain flavour submitted to the taste, and the heart of man, his moral sense, is quick to detect the absence in all other religious books of a certain savour which pervades the Bible, from Genesis, the book of beginnings, to the Apocalyptic announcements of the quick coming of the King.

And in the possession of this mysterious attribute, the Old and New Testaments are one. You cannot say there is more of it in the glowing paragraphs of the Apostle Paul than in the splendid prophecies and appeals of the great evangelic prophet, Isaiah. It is certainly in the Gospels, but it is not less in the story of the Exodus.

Throughout there is silence on topics which merely gratify curiosity, but on which other professed revelations have been copiously full. Throughout, there is no attempt to give instruction on science or nature, but to bend all energy in discussing the claims of God on men. Throughout, the crimson cord of sacrifice is clearly manifest, on which the books are strung together as beads upon a thread.

And throughout, there is ever the subtle, mysterious, ineffable quality called Inspiration, a term which is explained by the majestic words of this opening verse, "God, having spoken of old to the fathers, has at the end of these days spoken to us."

Scripture is the speech of God to man. It is this which gives it its unity. "The Lord, the mighty

God, has spoken, and called the earth." The writers may differ; but the inspiring mind is the same. The instruments may vary; but in every case the same theme is being played by the same master-hand. We should read the Bible as those who listen to the very speech of God. Well may it be called "the Word of God."

But the Scripture is God's speech in man. The heavenly treasure is in vessels of earth. "He spoke to the fathers in the prophets. . . He has spoken unto us in His Son." It is very remarkable to study the life of Jesus, and to listen to His constant statements as to the source of His marvellous words.

So utterly had He emptied Himself, that He originated nothing from Himself, but lived by the Father, in the same way as we are to live by Him. He distinctly declared that the words He spoke, He spoke not of Himself, but that words and works alike were the outcome of the Father, who dwelt within. Through those lips of clay the eternal God was speaking. Well might He also be called "the Word of God"!

And here the words of the prophets in the Old Testament are levelled up to the plane of the words of Jesus in the New. Without staying to make the least distinction, our writer tells us, under the teaching of the Spirit, that He who spoke in the one spoke also in the other.

Let us then think with equal reverence of the Old Testament as of the New. It was our Saviour's Bible. It was the food which Jesus loved, and lived upon. He was content to fast from all other food, if only He might have this. It was His one supreme appeal in conflict with the devil, and in the clinching of His arguments and exhortations with men.

And here we discover the reason. The voice of God spoke in the prophets, whose very name likens them to the up-rush of the geyser from its hidden source.

As God spoke in men, it is clear that He left them to express His thoughts in the language, and after the method, most familiar to them. They will speak of Nature just as they have been accustomed to find her. They will use the mode of speech whether poem or prose which is most habitual to their cast of thought. They will make allusions to the events transpiring around them, so as to be easily understood by their fellows.

But, whilst thus left to express God's thoughts in their own way, yet most certainly the divine Spirit must have carefully superintended their utterances, so that their words should accurately convey His messages to men.

In many parts of the Bible there is absolute dictation, word for word. In others, there is divine superintendence guarding from error, and guiding in the selection and arrangement of materials, as when Daniel quotes from historic records, and Moses embodies the sacred stories which his mother had taught him beside the flowing Nile.

In all, there is the full inspiration of the Spirit of God, by whom all Scripture has been given. Holy men spoke as they were moved by the Holy Spirit, . . . searching what, or what manner of time, the Spirit of Christ which was in them did signify" (2 Tim. 3.16 ; 2 Pet. 1. 20, 21; 1 Pet.

2.2).

We need not deny that other men have been illuminated, but the difference between illumination and inspiration is as far as the east is from the west. Nor do we say that God has not spoken in other men, or in these men at other times, but we do say that only in the Bible has God given the supreme revelation of His will, and the authoritative rule of our faith and practice.

The heart of man bears witness to this. We know that there is a tone in these words which is heard in no other voice. The upper chords of this instrument give it a timbre which none other can rival.

The revelation in the Old Testament was given in fragments (or portions). This is the meaning of the word rendered in the Old Version sundry times, and in the Revised divers portions. It refers, not to the successive ages over which it was spread, but to the numerous "portions" into which it was broken up. No one prophet could speak out all the truth. Each was entrusted with one or two syllables in the mighty sentences of God's speech.

At the best the view caught of God, and given to men through the prophets, though true, was partial and limited. But in Jesus there is nothing of this piecemeal revelation. "In him dwells all the fullness of the Godhead bodily." (Colossians 2.9). He has revealed the Father. Whosoever has seen Him has seen God, and to hear His words is to get the full-orbed revelation of the Infinite.

The earlier revelation was in many forms. The earthquake, the fire, the tempest, and the still small voice - each had its ministry. Symbol and parable, vision and metaphor, type and historic foreshadowing, all in turn served the divine end, like the ray which is broken into many prismatic hues. But in Jesus there is the steady shining of the pure ray of His glory, one uniform and invariable method of revelation.

Oh the matchless and glorious Book, the Word of God to men - to us, revealing not only God, but ourselves, explaining moods for which we had no cipher, touching us as no other book can, and in moments when all voices beside wax faint and still, telling facts which we have not been able to discover, but which we instantly recognise as truth; the bread of the soul, the key of life, disclosing more depths as we climb higher in Christian experience. We have tested you too long to doubt that you are what Jesus said you were, the indispensable and precious gift of God.

CHAPTER 2: THE DIGNITY OF CHRIST

"Who being the brightness of His glory, and the express image of His person, and upholding all things by the word of His power, when He had by Himself purged our sins, sat down on the right hand of the Majesty on high. Being made so much better than the angels." (Hebrews 1.3-4).

In these few lines we can but lightly touch on the majestic titles which a loving and adoring heart here heaps around the name of Jesus Christ, our Lord. The theme might well engage a seraph's tongue!

Yet our hearts may glow with ardour of the same nature, if not of the same amount. And perhaps we may be conscious of elements of rapture which the sons of light may never know, because of His near kinship to us. "My heart overflows with a goodly matter: I speak the things which I have made touching the King" (Psalm 45.1).

SON. --- " He has spoken to us in His Son." God has many sons, but only one Son. When, on the morning of His resurrection, our Lord met the frightened women, He said, "I ascend unto My Father and your Father, and My God and your God." But, as He used the words, they meant infinitely more of Himself than they could ever mean of man, however saintly or childlike. No creature-wing shall ever avail to carry us across the abyss which separates all created from all uncreated life.

But we may reverently accept the fact, so repeatedly emphasised, that Jesus is "the only begotten Son, which is in the bosom of the Father" (John 1.18). He is Son in a sense altogether unique.

This term, as used by our Lord, and as understood by the Jews, not only signified divine relationship, but divine equality. Hence, on one occasion, the Jews sought to kill him, because He said that God was His own Father, making Himself equal with God (John 5.18). And He, so far from correcting the opinion - as He must have done instantly, had it been erroneous - went on to confirm it and to substantiate its truthfulness.

The impression which Jesus of Nazareth left on all who knew Him was that of His extreme humility, but here was a point in which He could not abate one jot or tittle of His claims, lest He should be false to His knowledge of Himself, and to the repeated voice of God.

And so He died, because He affirmed, amid the assumed horror of His judges, that He was the Christ, the Son of God. "He counted it not a prize to be on an equality with God." (Philippians 2.6). It was His right.

His dignity is still further elaborated in the words which follow. He is THE BEAM OF THE DIVINE GLORY, for so might the word translated effulgence be rendered.

We have never seen the sun, but only its far-travelled ray, which left its surface some few minutes before. But the ray is of the same constitution as the orb from which it comes; if you unravel its texture, you will learn something of the very nature of the sun; they live in perpetual and glorious unity.

And as we consider the intimacy of that union, we are reminded of those familiar words, which tell us that though no man has seen God at any time, yet He has been revealed in the Word made flesh. We hear our Master saying again the old, deep, mysterious words: "I and my Father are one. We will come and make our abode." (John 10.30; 14.23). And we can sympathise with the evening hymn of the early Church, sung around the shores of the Bosphorus:

"Hail! gladdening Light, of His pure glory poured,
Who is the Immortal Father, Heavenly, Blest."
He is also THE IMPRESS OF THE DIVINE NATURE. The allusion here is to the impression

made by a seal on molten wax; and as the image made on the wax is the exact resemblance, though on another substance, of the die, so is Christ the exact resemblance of the Father in our human flesh. And thus He was able to say, "He who has seen me has seen the Father" (John 14.9).

The Life of Jesus is the Life of God rendered into the terms of our human life, so that we may understand the very being and nature of God by seeing it reproduced before us, so far as it is possible, in the character and life of Jesus. These two images complete each other.

You might argue from the first, that as the ray is only part of the sun, so Christ is only part of God, but this mistake is corrected by the second, for an impression must be coextensive with the seal.

You might argue from the second, that as the impression might be made on a very inferior material, so Christ's nature was a very unworthy vehicle of the divine glory, but this mistake is corrected by the first, for a beam is of the same texture as the sun. Coextensive with God, of the same nature as God, thus is Jesus Christ.

He is, therefore, superior to angels (verse 4). Lofty as was the esteem in which Hebrew believers had been wont to hold those bright and blessed spirits, they were not for a moment to be compared with Him whose majestic claims are the theme of these glowing words.

He surpasses them in the glory of Divine Nature. Turn to Psalm 2 - one of the grandest miniature dramas in all literature. Probably composed concerning some marked episode in the reign of David, there is a glow, a sublimity, in the diction which no earthly monarch could exhaust. We are not, therefore, surprised to find the early Church applying it to Christ (Acts 4.25).

In reading it, we first hear the roar of the mob and the calm decision of the throne; and then our attention is centred on Him who comes forward, bearing the divine autograph to the decree which declares Him Son. Nothing like this was ever said to angel, however exalted in character or devoted in service. It is only befitting, then, that the unsinning sons of light should worship Him; and as we hear the command issued, "Let all the angels of God worship Him," we are still further impressed by the immense distance between their nature and His.

Do we worship Him enough? During His earthly life He was constantly met by expressive acts of homage, which, unlike Peter in the house of Cornelius, He did not repress. The almost instinctive act of the little group, from which He was parted on the Mount of Olives in His ascension, was to worship Him (Luke 24.52).

And no sooner had He passed to His home than there burst from the Church a tide of adoration which has only become wider and deeper with the ages. The Epistles, and especially the Book of Revelation, teem with expressions of worship to Christ. And the death-cries of martyrs must have familiarised the heathen mind with the homage paid to Christ by Christians.

Of the worship offered Him in catacombs, or in their secret meetings, amongst dens and caves, paganism was necessarily ignorant. But the behaviour and exclamations of the servants of Jesus, arraigned before heathen tribunals, and exposed to the most agonising deaths, were matters of public notoriety.

Some years ago, beneath the ruins of the Palatine palace, was discovered a rough sketch, traced in all probability by the hand of a pagan slave in the second century. A human figure, with the head of an ass, is represented as fixed to the cross; while another figure, in a tunic, stands on one side, making a gesture which was the customary pagan expression of adoration. Underneath this caricature ran the inscription, rudely written, Alexamenos adores his God. But what a tribute to the worship paid in those early days to our Saviour, amidst gibes and taunts and persecution!

The hymns which have come down to us ring with the same spirit. Pliny writes to tell the Emperor that the Christians of Asia Minor were accustomed to meet to sing praise to Christ as God. As each morning broke, the believer of those primitive days repeated in private the Gloria in Excelsis as his hymn of supplication and praise: "You only are holy, You only are the Lord, You only, Oh Christ, with the Holy Spirit, are most high in the glory of God the Father."

The early Church did not simply admire Christ, it adored Him.

Is not this a great lack in our private devotions? We are so apt to concentrate our thoughts on ourselves, and to thank for what we have received. We do not sufficiently often forget our own petty wants and anxieties, and launch down our tiny rivulet, until we are borne out into the great ocean of praise, which is ever breaking in music around the person of Jesus.

Praise is one of the greatest acts of which we are capable, and it is most like the service of heaven. There they ask for naught, for they have all and abound, but throughout the cycles of glory the denizens of those bright worlds fill them with praise.

And why should not earthly tasks be wrought to the same music? We are the priests of creation. It becomes us to gather up and express the sentiments which are mutely dumb, but which await our offering at the altar of God.

Let a part of our private and public devotion be ever dedicated to the praise of Jesus, when we shall break forth into some hymn, or psalm, or spiritual song, singing and praising Christ with angels and archangels and all the hosts of the redeemed. On that brow, once thorn-crowned, let us entwine our laurels. Upon that ear, once familiarised with threats and scorn, let us pour the fullness of our adoring devotion. So shall we gain and give new thoughts of the supreme dignity of the Lord Jesus. "You are worthy to receive ... honour."

CHAPTER 3: THE GLORY OF CHRIST'S OFFICE

"He has by inheritance obtained a more excellent name." (Hebrews 1.4).

Apart from Scripture, we would have been disposed to infer the existence of other orders of intelligent and spiritual beings besides man. As the order of creation climbs up to man from the lowest living organism through many various stages of existence, so surely the series must be continued beyond man, through rank on rank of spiritual existence up to the very steps of the eternal throne. The divine mind must be as prolific in spiritual as it has been in natural forms of life.

But we are not left to conjecture. From every part of Scripture come testimonies to the existence of angels. They rejoiced when the world was made, and they are depicted as ushering in with songs that new creation for which we long. They stood sentries at the gate of a lost paradise; and at each of the twelve gates of the New Jerusalem an angel stands (Revelation 21.12).

They trod the plains of Mamre, and sang over the fields of Bethlehem. One prepared the meal on the desert sands for Elijah, another led Peter out of gaol and a third flashed through the storm to stand by the hammock where the Apostle Paul was sleeping (Acts 27.23,24).

But in the mind of the pious Hebrew the greatest work which the angels ever wrought was in connection with the giving of the law. The children of Israel received the law "as it was ordained by angels" (Acts 7.53, R.V.). It was necessary, therefore, in showing the superiority of the Gospel to the Law, to begin by showing the superiority of Him through whom the Gospel was given, over all orders of bright and blessed spirits, which, in their shining ranks and their twenty thousand chariots, went and came during the giving of the decalogue from the brow of Sinai (Psalm 68.17).

It is not difficult to prove the Lord's superiority to angels. It is twofold: in Nature and in Office.

In Nature "He has by inheritance obtained a more excellent name than they" (verse 4). In verse 7, quoted from Psalm 104.4 (R.V. marg.), where they are distinctly spoken of as messengers and ministers, they are compared to winds and flames, winds for their swiftness and invisibility, flames because of their ardent love.

But how great the gulf between their nature, which may thus be compared to the elements of creation, and the nature of that glorious Being whom they are bidden to worship, and Who is addressed in the sublime title of Son! (Hebrews 1.6; Psalm 97.7.)

In verse 14 they are spoken of as ministering spirits, "sent forth to do service for the sake of those who will inherit salvation" (R.V.). This liturgy of service is a literal fact. When struggling against overwhelming difficulties, when walking the dark, wild mountain-pass alone, when in peril or urgent need - we are surrounded by invisible forms, like those which accompanied the path of Jesus, ministering to Him in the desert, strengthening Him in the garden, hovering around His cross, watching His grave and accompanying Him to his home.

They keep pace with the swiftest trains in which we travel. They come unsoiled through the murkiest air. They smooth away the heaviest difficulties. They garrison with light the darkest sepulchres. They bear us up in their hands, lest we should strike our foot against a stone.

Many an escape from imminent peril; many an unexpected assistance; many a bright and holy thought whispered in the ear, we know not whence or how - is due to those bright and loving spirits.

"The good Lord forgive me," says Bishop Hall, "for that, amongst my other offences, I have suffered myself so much to forget the presence of His holy angels." But valuable as their office is, it is not to be mentioned in the same breath as Christ's, which is set down for us in this chapter.

He Is The Organ of Creation. "By whom also He made the worlds." To make that which is seen out of nothing, that is creation: it is a divine work; and creation is attributed to Christ. "By him were all things created that are in heaven and that are in earth." "All things were made by him; and without him was not anything made that was made" (Colossians 1.16; John 1.3).

But the word here and in 11. 3 translated 'worlds' means 'ages'. Not only was the material universe made by Him, but each of the great ages of the world's story has been instituted by Jesus Christ.

When genius aspires to immortality, it leaves the artist's name inscribed on stone or canvas: and so Inspiration, "dipping her pen in indelible truth, inscribes the name of Jesus on all we see - on sun and stars, flower and tree, rock and mountain, the unstable waters and the firm land; and also on what we do not see, nor shall, until death has removed the veil - on angels and spirits, on the city and heavens of the eternal world."

This thought comes out clearly in the sublime quotation made in verse 10 from Psalm 102. That inspired poem is obviously inscribed to Yahweh. "You, Yahweh, in the beginning have laid the foundation of the earth, and the heavens are the work of Your hands." But here, without the least apology, or hint of accommodating the words to an inferior use, it is applied directly to Christ. Mark the certainty of this inspired man that Jesus is Yahweh! How sure of the Deity of his Lord! And what a splendid tribute to His immutability!

Mark how the Epistle rings with the unchangeableness of Jesus, in His human love (13.8), in His priesthood (7. 24), and here in His divine nature (vv. 10-12).

We live in a world of change. The earth is not the same today as it was ages ago, or as it will be ages on. The sun is radiating off its heat. The moon no longer as of yore burns and glows; she is but an immense opaque cinder, reflecting the sunlight from her disk. Stars have burnt out, and will. The universe is waxing old, as garments which from perpetual use become threadbare.

But the wearing out of the garment is no proof of the waning strength or slackening energy of the wearer. Nay, when garments wear out quickest, it is generally the time of robustest youth or manhood. You wrap up and lay aside your clothes when they have served their purpose; but you are the same in the new suit as in the old.

Creation is the vesture of Christ. He wraps himself about in its ample folds. Its decay affects Him not. And, when He shall have laid it all aside, and replaced it by the new heavens and the new earth, He will be the same for evermore.

With what new interest may we not now turn to the archaic record, which tells how God created the heavens and the earth. Those sublime syllables, "Light, be!" were spoken by the voice that trembled in dying anguish on the cross. Rolling rivers, swelling seas, waving woods, bursting flowers, carolling birds, innumerable beasts, stars sparkling like diamonds on the pavilion of night - all newly made, all throbbing with God's own life, and all very good. But, mainly and gloriously, all the work of those hands which were nailed helplessly to the cross, which itself, as well as the iron that pierced Him, was the result of His creative will.

He Is The God of Providence. "Upholding all things by the word of His power" (verse 3). He is the prop which underpins creation. Christ, and not fate. Christ, and not nature. Christ, and not abstract impersonal law.

Law is but the invariable method of His working. "In Him all things live, and move, and have their being." "By him all things consist." (Acts 17.28; Colossians 1.17). He is ever at work repeating on the large scale of creation the deeds of His earthly life. And if He did not do them, they must be forever undone.

At His word rainwater and dew become grape-juice; tiny handfuls of grain fill the autumn barns, storms die away into calm, fish are led through the paths of the sea, rills are sent among the mountains, and stars are maintained in their courses, so that "not one fails."

All power is given to Him in heaven and on earth. Why, then, are you so sad? Your best Friend is the Lord of Providence. Your Brother is Prime Minister of the universe, and holds the keys of the divine commissariat. Go to Him with the empty sacks of your need. He will not only fill them, but fill them freely, without money and without price, as Joseph did in the old story of the days of the Pharaohs.

He Is The Saviour of Sinners. "He purged our sins." We shall have many opportunities of dwelling on this glorious fact. Jesus is Saviour, Redeemer, and the High-Priest. This is His proudest title; in this work no angel or created spirit can bear Him rivalry. In the work of salvation He is alone. No angel could atone for sin, or plead our cause, or emancipate us from the thrall of evil.

But notice the finality of this act. "He made purging of sins " (see Greek). It is finished, forever complete, done irrevocably and finally. If only we are one with Him by a living faith, our sins, which were many, are washed out; as an inscription from a slate, as a stain from a robe, as a cloud from the azure of heaven.

Gone as a stone into the bottomless abyss! Gone, never to confront us here or hereafter! "Who is He Who condemns? It is Christ that died, yes, rather, Who is risen again, Who is even at the right hand of God; who also makes intercession for us" (Romans 8. 34).

He Is Also King. And on what does His kingdom rest? What is the basis of that Royalty of which we constantly sing, in the noble words of the primitive Church? "You are the King of Glory, 0h Christ." It is a double basis.

He is King by right of His divine nature. "Your throne, O God, is for ever and ever." Well might Psalm 45 be entitled the poem of the lilies, as if to denote its pure and choice and matchless beauties. It celebrated the marriage of Solomon, but, after the manner of those inspired singers, its authors soon passed from the earthly to the heavenly, from the transient type of the earthly realm to the eternal and imperishable realities of the divine royalty of Christ.

He is also King as the reward of His obedience unto death. "He became obedient to death, even the death of the cross, wherefore, God also has highly exalted Him" (Philippians 2. 8,9).

Satan offered Him sovereignty in return for one act of homage, and Christ refused, and descended the mountain to poverty and shame and death, but through these things He has won for Himself a Kingdom which is yet in its infancy, but is destined to stand when all the kingdoms of this world have crumbled to dust.

As Christ emerged from the cross and the grave, where He had purged our sins, it seemed as if words were addressed to Him which David had caught ages before: "The LORD said to my Lord, Sit on my right hand, until I make Your enemies Your footstool" (verse 13; Psalm 110. 1). This is the interpretation which the Apostle Peter, in the flush of Pentecostal inspiration, put on these words (Acts 2. 34). And, accordingly, we are told, "He was received up into heaven, and sat on the right hand of God " (Mark 16. 19). "He sat down on the right hand of the Majesty on high" (verse 3).

"He sat down." Love is regnant. The Lamb is in the midst of the Throne. Behold His majesty, and worship Him with angels and archangels, and all the throng of the redeemed. Prostrate yourself at His feet, consecrating to Him all you are and all you have.

Comfort yourself also by remembering that He would not sit to rest from His labours in redemption, and in the purging away of sins, unless they were so completely finished that there was nothing more to do. It is all accomplished; and it is all very good. He has ceased from His works, because they are done; and therefore He is entered into his rest.

And that word "until" is full of hope. God speaks it, and encourages us to expect the time when He shall have put down all rule and all authority and power; and when death itself, the last enemy, shall be destroyed (1 Corinthians 15. 24-26).

CHAPTER 4: DRIFTING

"We ought to give the more earnest heed to the things which we have heard, lest at any time we should let them slip." - (HEBREWS 2. 1).

SALVATION is a great word, and it is one of the keywords of this Epistle. Heirs of salvation (1.14), so great salvation (2.3), Captain of salvation (2.10), eternal salvation (5. 9), things that accompany salvation (6.9), salvation to the uttermost (7.25), and His appearance the second time without sin unto salvation (ix. 28).

Sometimes it is salvation from the penalty of sin that is spoken of. The past tense is then used of that final and blessed act by which, through faith in the blood of Jesus, we are forever placed beyond fear of judgment and punishment; so that we are to the windward of the storm, which spent itself on the head of our Substitute and representative on Calvary, and can therefore never break on us. "By grace have you been saved through faith" (Ephesians 2.8, R.V).

Sometimes it is salvation from the power of sin. The present tense is then employed, of the long and gradual process by which we are set free from evil, which has worked itself so deeply into our system. "To us who are being saved the word of the cross is the power of God" (1 Corinthians 1.18, R.V). Sometimes salvation from all physical and other evils is implied. The future tense is then summoned into requisition, painting its splendid frescoes on the mists that hang so densely before our view, and telling us of resurrection in our Saviour's likeness and presentation in His home, faultless, with exceeding joy. "We know that when He shall appear we shall be like Him, for we shall see Him as he is" (1 John 3. 2). "Now is our salvation nearer than when we believed. The night is far spent; the day is at hand" (Romans 13. 11).

In the above passage the word "salvation" includes the entire process, from its beginning to its end; though perhaps it is especially tinctured with the first thought mentioned above. And if we follow out the figure suggested by the rendering of the first verse of this chapter in the Revised Version, we may compare salvation to a great harbour, past which we are in danger of drifting through culpable neglect.

"We ought to give the more earnest heed to the things that were heard, lest haply we drift away from them." "How shall we escape if we neglect so great salvation!"

CONSIDER GOD'S SCHEME OF SALVATION AS A GREAT HARBOUR. - After a wild night, we have gone down to the harbour, over whose arms the angry waves have been dashing with boom of thunder and in clouds of spray. Outside, the sea has been tossing and churning, the cloud bank driving hurriedly across the sky, the winds howling like the furies of olden fable. But within those glorious walls, the barks which had put in during the night were riding in safety; the sailors resting, or repairing rents in sail and tackle, whilst the waters were unstirred by the storm raging without. Such a refuge or harbour is a fit emblem of salvation, where tempest-driven souls find shelter and peace.

It is great in its sweep. Sufficient to embrace a ruined world. Room in it for whole navies of souls to ride at anchor. Space enough for every ship of Adam's race launched from the shores of time. "He is the propitiation for the whole world." "Whosoever will."

Already it is becoming filled. There a vessel once manned by seven devils, a pirate ship, but captured by our Emmanuel, and at her stem the name, Mary of Magdala. And here one dismasted, and almost shattered, rescued from the fury of the maelstrom at the last hour; on her stem the words, The Dying Thief. And there another, long employed in efforts to sap the very walls of the harbour, and now flying a pennon from the masthead, Chief of Sinners and Least of Saints. And all around a forest of masts, "a multitude which no man can number, of all nations, and kindreds, and peoples, and tongues."

It is great in its foundations. The chief requisite in constructing a sea-wall is to get a foundation which can stand unmoved amid the heaviest seas. The shifting sand must be pierced down to the granite rock. But this harbour has foundations mighty enough to inspire strong consolation in those who have fled to it for refuge; the promise, and as if that were not enough, the oath, of God (Hebrews 6.17, 18). Hark, how the storm of judgment is rising out there at sea! "If the foundations be destroyed, what shall the righteous do?" (Psalm 11.3). Fear not! there is no room for alarm. The waves may wash off some mussel-shells, or tear away the green sea-lichen which has encrusted the mouldings on the walls, but it would be easier to dig out the everlasting hills from their base than make one stone in those foundations start.

It was great in its cost. By the tubular bridge over the Menai Straits stands a column, which records the names of those who perished during the construction of that great triumph of engineering skill. Nothing is said of the money spent, only of the lives sacrificed. And so, beside the harbour of our salvation, near to its mouth, so as to be read by every ship entering its enclosure, rises another column, with this as its inscription: "Sacred to the memory of the Son of God, who gave His life a sacrifice for the sin of the world."

It seems an easy thing to be saved: "Look to me, and be you saved." (Isaiah 45.22). But we do not always remember how much happened before it became so easy - the agony and bloody sweat; the cross and passion; the precious death and burial.

It has been great in its announcement. The Jews thought much of their Law, because of the majesty of its proclamation. Spoken from the inaccessible cliffs of Sinai, with its beetling crags, its red sandstone peaks bathed in fire, while thunders and lightnings, thick clouds and trumpet-notes, were the sublime accessories of the scene.

It was the authorised belief also among the Jews that the Law was given through angels (Deuteronomy 23.2 ; Acts 7.53; Gal. 3.19 ; Hebrews 2.2). And the thought that these strong and sinless beings were the medium of the Almighty's will served, in the eyes of all devout Hebrews, to enhance the sanctity and glory of the Law.

Compared with this, how simple the accessories of the words of Jesus! Spoken in sweet and gentle tones, falling as the soft showers on the tender grass, and distilling quietly as the dew, not frightening the most sinful, nor startling little babes, they stole as the melody from silver bells, borne on a summer wind into the ears of men. The boat or hill slope His pulpit, the poor His audience,the common incidents of nature or life His text.

But in reality there was a vast difference. The announcement of the Law was by angels. The announcement of the Gospel was by the Son. If the one were august, what must not the other have been! If the one were made sure by the most tremendous sanctions, what should not be said of the other! Proclaimed by the Lord, confirmed by Apostles and eyewitnesses, testified to by the Almighty Himself, in signs and wonders, and gifts of the Holy Spirit. How dare we treat it with contumely or neglect?

Or, if we do, shall not our penalty be in proportion to the magnitude of our offence? "If the word spoken through angels proved steadfast, and every transgression and disobedience received a just recompense of reward, how shall we escape, if we neglect so great salvation?" "Therefore we ought to give the more earnest heed to the things that were heard, lest haply we drift away from them."

It will be great in its penalties. The tendency of our age is to minimise God's righteous judgment on sin. It seems to be prevalently thought that, because our dispensation is one of love and mercy, therefore there is the less need to dread the results of sin. But the inspired writer here argues in a precisely contrary sense. Just because this age is one of such tender mercy, therefore sins against its King are more deadly, and the penalties heavier.

In the old days no transgression, - positive, - and no disobedience, - negative, - escaped its just recompense of reward; and in these days there is even less likelihood of their doing so. The word spoken by the Son is even more steadfast, i.e. effective to secure the infliction of the punishment it announces, than the word of angels. My readers, beware! "He that despised Moses' law died without mercy under two or three witnesses; of how much sorer punishment shall he be thought worthy who hath trodden under foot the Son of God!" (10.28,29).

THE DANGER TO WHICH WE ARE MOST EXPOSED. - "Lest haply we drift away" (2.2, R.V.). For every one that definitely turns his back on Christ, there are hundreds who drift from Him. Life's ocean is full of currents, any one of which will sweep us past the harbour-mouth even when we seem nearest to it, and carry us far out to sea.

It is the drift that ruins men. The drift of the religious world. The drift of old habits and associations; which, in the case of these Hebrew Christians, was setting so strongly toward Judaism, bearing them back to the religious system from which they had come out. The drift of one's own evil nature, always chafing to bear us from God to that which is earthly and sensuous. The drift of the pressure of temptation.

The young man coming from a pious home does not distinctly and deliberately say, "I renounce my father's God." But he finds himself with a set of business associates who have no care for religion; and, after a brief struggle, he relaxes his efforts and begins to drift, until the coastline of heaven recedes so far into the dim distance that he is doubtful if he ever really saw it.

The business man who now shamelessly follows the lowest maxims of his trade was once upright and high-minded. He would have blushed to think it possible for such things to be done by him. But he began by yielding in very trivial points to the strong pressure of competition; and when once he had allowed himself to be caught by the tide, it bore him far beyond his first intention.

The professing Christian who now scarcely pretends to open the Bible or pray came to so terrible a position, not at a single leap, but by yielding to the pressure of the constant waywardness of the old nature, and thus drifted into an arctic region, where he is likely to perish, benumbed and frozen, unless rescued, and launched on the warm gulf-stream of the love of God.

It is so easy, and so much pleasanter, to drift. Just to lie back, and renounce effort, and let yourself go whither the waters will, as they break musically on the sides of the rocking boat. But, ah, how ineffable the remorse, how disastrous the result!

Are you drifting? You can easily tell. Are you conscious of effort, of daily, hourly resistance to the stream around you, and within? Do the things of God and heaven loom more clearly on your vision? Do the waters foam angrily at your prow as you force your way through them?

If so, rejoice! but remember that only divine strength can suffice to maintain the conflict, and keep the boat's head against the stream. If not, you are drifting. Hail the strong Son of God! Ask Him to come on board, and stay you, and bring you into port.

AN UNANSWERABLE QUESTION. "How shall we escape, if we neglect?" The sailor who refuses lifeboat and harbour does not escape. The self-murderer who tears the bandages from his wounds does not escape. The physician who ridicules ordinary precautions against plague does not escape. "How then shall we escape?"

Did the Israelite escape who refused to sprinkle the blood upon the doorposts of his house? Did the man who gathered sticks on the Sabbath-day escape, although he might have pleaded that it was the first offence? Did the prince who had taken the Moabitess to wife escape, though he bore a high rank? Did Moses and Aaron escape, though they were the leaders of the people? No! None of these escaped. "Every transgression and disobedience received its just recompense of reward." "How then shall we escape?"

Is it likely that we should escape? We have neglected the only Name given under heaven among men by which we can be saved. We have added contumely to neglect in refusing that which it has cost God so much to give. We have flouted His only Son, our Lord; and our disrespect to Him cannot be a small crime in the eye of the Infinite Father. "How shall we escape?"

No, if you neglect (and notice, that to neglect is to reject), there is no escape. You will not escape the storms of sorrow, of temptation, or of the righteous judgment of God. You will not escape the deserved and necessary punishment of your sins. You will not escape the worm which never dies, nor the fire which is never quenched. Out there, shelterless amid the rage of the sea, or yonder, driven to pieces on the rocks, you will be wrecked, and go down with all hands on board, never sighted by the heavenly watchers, nor welcomed into the harbour of the saints' everlasting rest.

Chapter 5: "WHAT IS MAN?"

"We see Jesus, ... crowned with glory and honour." {HEBREWS 2.5-9).

IN the first great division of this treatise, we have seen the incomparable superiority of the Lord Jesus to angels, and archangels, and all the heavenly host. But now there arises an objection which was very keenly realised by these Hebrew Christians, and which, to a certain extent, presses upon us all. Why did the Son of God become man? How are the sorrows, sufferings, and death of the Man of Nazareth consistent with the sublime glories of the Son of God, the equal and fellow of the Eternal?

These questions are answered during the remainder of the chapter, and may be gathered up into a single sentence. He who was above all angels became lower than the angels for a little time, that He might lift men from their abasement, and set them on His own glorious level in His heavenly

Father's kingdom, and that He might be a faithful and merciful High Priest for the sorrowful and tempted and dying.

Here is an act worthy of a God Here are reasons which are more than sufficient to answer the old question, for which Anselm prepared so elaborate a reply in his book, "Cur Deus Homo?"

"What is man?" Those three words in verse 6 are the fit starting point of the argument. We need not only a true philosophy of God, but a true philosophy of man, in order to right thinking on the Gospel.

The idolater thinks man inferior to birds and beasts and creeping things, before which he prostrates himself. The materialist reckons him to be the chance product of natural forces which have evolved him, and before which he is therefore likely to pass away. The pseudo-science of the time makes him of one blood with ape and gorilla, and assigns him a common origin with the beasts. See what gigantic systems of error have developed from mistaken conceptions of the true nature and dignity of man!

From all such we turn to that noble ideal of man's essential dignity, given in this sublime paragraph, which corrects our mistaken notions, and, whilst giving us an explanation that harmonises with all our experience and observation, opens up to us vistas of thought worthy of God.

MAN AS GOD MADE HIM. The description given here of the origin and dignity of man is taken from Psalm 8, which is doubtless a reminiscence of the days when David kept his father's sheep, even if it were not composed on that very spot over which in after-years the heavenly choirs broke upon the astonished shepherds "abiding in the field, keeping watch over their flock by night."

Turn to that Psalm, and see how well it expresses the emotions which must well up in devout hearts to God as we consider the midnight heavens, the tapestry work of His fingers, and the spheres lit by the moon and stars, which He has ordained. How impossible it is for those who are given to devout reflection to come in contact with any of the grander forms of natural beauty, the far-spread expanse of ocean, the outlines of the mountains, the changing pomp of the skies, without turning from the handiwork to the great Artisan, with some such expression as the apostrophe with which the Psalm opens and closes: "0h LORD, our Lord, how excellent is Your name in all the earth."

At first sight, man is utterly unworthy to be compared with those vast and wondrous spectacles revealed to us by the veiling of the sun. His life is but as a breath; as a shadow careering over the mountainside; as the existence of the aphides on a leaf in the vast forests of being.

What can be said of his character, sin-stained and befouled, in contrast with peaks whose virgin snows have never been defiled, with sylvan scenes, whose peace has never been ruffled, with silvery spheres, whose chimes of perfect harmony have never been broken by discord? Four times over is the question asked upon the pages of Scripture, "What is man, that You are mindful of him?" (Psalm 94.3; Job 7.17, 20; Psalm 8.4; Hebrews 2. 6).

Yet it is an undeniable fact that God is mindful of man, and that He does visit him.

"Mindful!" There is not a moment in God's existence in which He is not as mindful of this world of men as the mother of the babe whom she has left for a moment in the next room, but whose slightest cry or moan she is quick to catch. "I am poor and needy, yet the Lord thinks on me." "How precious are Your thoughts to me, Oh God!" (Psalm 40.17; 139.17).

"Visiting!" No cot is so lowly, no heart so wayward, no life so solitary, but God visits it. No one shall read these lines, the path around whose heart-door is not trodden hard by the feet of Him who often comes and stands and knocks. We speak as if only our sorrows were divine visitations. Alas for us, if it were only so! Every throb of holy desire, every gentle mercy, every gift of Providence, is a visitation of God.

But there must be some great and sufficient reason why the Maker of the universe should take so much interest in man. Evidently bigness is not greatness. A tiny babe is worth more than the tallest mountain, and an empress-mother will linger in the one room where her child is ill, though she forsake the remainder of her almost illimitable domain. What if earth shall turn out to be the nursery of the universe!

The true clue, however, to all speculation is to be found in the declaration by the Psalmist of God's original design in making man: "You crown him. ... You made him to have dominion. . . . You have put all things under his feet" (Psalm 8.5, 6 R.V.). Nor was this lofty ideal first given to the Psalmist's poetic vision. It had an earlier origin. It is a fragment of the great charter of humanity, which God gave to our first parents in Paradise.

Turn to that noble archaic record, Genesis 1.26-28, which transcends the imaginings of modern science as far as it does those legends of creation which make the heathen literature with which they are incorporated incredible.

Its simplicity, its sublimity, its fitness, attest its origin and authority to be divine. We are prepared to admit that God's work in creation was symmetrical and orderly, and that He worked out His design according to an ever-unfolding plan. But science has discovered nothing as yet to contradict the express statements of Scripture, that the first man was not at all inferior to ourselves in those intellectual and moral faculties which are the noblest heritage of mankind.

"God created man in His own image" (Genesis 1.27). - There we have the divine likeness. Our mental and moral nature is made on the same plan as God's, the divine in miniature. Truth, love, and purity, like the principles of mathematics, are the same in us as in Him.

If it were not so, we could not know or understand Him. But since it is so, it has been possible for Him to take on Himself our nature - possible also that we shall be one day transformed to the perfect image of His beauty.

"And God said, Have dominion" (Genesis 1.28). - There you have royal supremacy. Man was intended to be God's vice-regent and representative. King in a palace stored with all to please him, monarch and sovereign of all the lower orders of creation.

The sun to labour for him as a very Hercules, the moon to light his nights, or lead the waters round the earth in tides, cleansing his coasts, elements of nature to be his slaves and messengers; flowers to scent his path, fruits to please his taste, birds to sing for him, fish to feed him, beasts to toil for him and carry him.

Not a cringing slave, but a king crowned with the glory of rule, and with the honour of universal supremacy. Only a little lower than angels because they are not, like him, encumbered with flesh and blood. This is man as God made him to be.

MAN AS SIN HAS MADE HIM. "We see not yet all things subjected to him" (Hebrews 2.8 R.V.). His crown is rolled in the dust, his honour tarnished and stained. His sovereignty is strongly disputed by the lower orders of creation.

If trees nourish him, it is after strenuous care, and they often disappoint. If the earth supplies him with food, it is in tardy response to exhausting toil. If the beasts serve him, it is because they have been laboriously tamed and trained, whilst vast numbers roam the forest glades, setting him at defiance. If he catch the fish of the sea, or the bird of the air, he must wait long in cunning concealment.

Some traces of the old lordship are still apparent, in the terror which the sound of the human voice and the glance of the eye still inspire in the lower creatures, as in the feats of lion-tamer or snake-charmer. But for the most part anarchy and rebellion have laid waste man's fair realm.

So degraded has he become, that he has bowed before the objects that he was to command; and has prostrated his royal form in shrines dedicated to birds, and four-footed beasts, and creeping things. It is the fashion nowadays to extol heathen philosophy; but how can we compare it for a moment with the religion of the Bible, when its pyramids are filled with mummies of deified animals, and its temples with the sacred bull!

Where is the supremacy of man? Not in the savage cowering before the beasts of the forest; nor in the civilised races that are the slaves of lust and sensuality and swinish indulgence; nor in those who, refusing to recognise the authority of God, fail to exercise any authority themselves.

"Sin has reigned," as the Apostle says most truly (Romans 5.21). And all who bow their necks beneath its yoke are slaves and menials and cowering subjects, in comparison with what God made and meant them to be.

Do not point to the wretched groups surrounding the doors of the pubs and bars in the metropolis of the most Christian people of the world, and regard their condition as a stain on the love or power of God. This is not His work. These are the products of sin. 'An enemy has done this'.

Would you see man as God intended him to be, you must go back to Eden, or forward to the New Jerusalem. Sin defiles, debases, disfigures, and blasts all it touches. And we may shudder to think that its virus is working through our frame, as we discover the results of its ravages upon myriads around.

MAN AS CHRIST CAN MAKE HIM. "We behold Jesus crowned with glory and honour" (verse 9). "What help is that?" cries an objector; "of course He is crowned with glory and honour, since He is the Son of God."

But notice, the glory and honour mentioned here are altogether different from the glory of Hebrews 1. 3. That was the incommunicable glory of His deity. This is the acquired glory of His humanity.

In John 17 our Lord himself distinguishes between the two. In verse 5, the glory which He had with the Father as His right before all worlds. In verse 24, the glory given as the reward for His sufferings, which He could not have had unless He had taken upon Himself the form of a servant, and had been made in the fashion of man, humbling Himself, and becoming obedient to the death of the cross, "made a little lower than the angels, because of the suffering of death; crowned with glory and honour, that He, by the grace of God, should taste death for every man" (Phil 2.7, 8; Hebrews 2.10).

This is the crown wherewith His Father crowned Him in the day of the gladness of His heart, when, as man, He came forth victorious from the last wrestle with the Prince of Hell. All through His earthly life He fulfilled the ancient ideal of man. He was God's image, and those who saw Him saw the Father. He was Sovereign in His commands.

Winds and waves did His bidding. Trees withered at His touch. Fish in shoals obeyed His will. Droves of cattle fled before His scourge of small cords. Disease and death and devils owned Hs sway. But all was more fully realised when He was about to return to His Father, and said, in a noble outburst of conscious supremacy, "All power is given unto Me in heaven and in earth."

"We behold Him" Behold him, Christian reader! The wreaths of empire are on His brow. The keys of death and Hades swing at His girdle. The mysterious living creatures, representatives of redeemed creation, attest that He is worthy. All things in heaven and earth, and under the earth, and in the seas, worship Him, so do the bands of angels, beneath whom He stooped for a little season, on our behalf.

And as He is, we too shall be He is there as the type and specimen and representative of redeemed men. We are linked with Him in indissoluble union. Through Him we shall get back our lost empire. We too shall be crowned with glory and honour.

The day is not far distant when we shall sit at His side-joint-heirs in His empire; comrades in His glory, as we have been comrades in His sorrows; beneath our feet all things visible and invisible, thrones and principalities and powers, whilst above us shall be the unclouded empyrean of our Father's love, forever and forever. Oh, destiny of surpassing bliss! Oh, rapture of saintly hearts! Oh, miracle of divine omnipotence!

CHAPTER 6: "PERFECT THROUGH SUFFERINGS"

"It became Him, for Whom are all things, and by Whom are all things, in bringing many sons unto glory, to make the Captain of their salvation perfect through sufferings." (HEBREWS 2.10).

THERE is no book which can stand the test of sorrow and suffering as the Bible can. Other books may delight us in sunny hours, when the heart is gay; but in dark and overcast days we fling them aside, and eagerly betake ourselves to our Bibles. And the reason for this lies in the fact that this Book was born in the fires. It is soaked with the tears, either of those who wrote or of those addressed.

Take, for instance, this Epistle. It was intended to solace the bitter anguish of these Hebrew Christians, who were exposed to the double fury of the storm.

In the first place, there was the inevitable opposition and persecution to be encountered by all followers of the Nazarene, not only from the Gentiles, but especially from their fellow-countrymen, who accounted them apostates.

Next, there was the pain of excommunication from the splendid rites of the Temple, with its daily service, its solemn feasts, its magnificent ceremonial. Only those amongst ourselves who from childhood have been wont to worship in some splendid minster, with its pealing organ, full-voiced choir, and mystery of architecture, arresting and enchaining every sense of beauty, but who have felt constrained to join the worship of an obscure handful in some plain meetinghouse, can realise how painfully those who were addressed in these words missed the religious associations of their early days.

And then this suffering, thorn-crowned, dying Messiah! It seemed almost impossible to realise that He was the Christ of national desire. The objections that baffled the faith of the two travellers to Emmaus arose in almost irresistible force: "The chief priests and our rulers have crucified Him, but we trusted that it had been He which should have redeemed Israel" (Luke 24. 20).

No attempt is made in these words to minimise the sufferings of Christ. That were impossible and superfluous. He is King in the realm of sorrow; peerless in His pain; supreme in His distress. Though earth be full of sufferers, none can vie with our Lord in His.

Human nature is limited. The confines of its joys or sorrows are soon touched. The pendulum swings only hither and thither. But who shall estimate the capacity of Christ's nature? And because of it, He could taste the sweets of a joy beyond His fellows, and of sorrow so excessive as to warrant the challenge: "Behold, and see if there be any sorrow like unto my sorrow, with which the Lord has afflicted me in the day of His fierce anger." (Lamentations 1.12).

If it be true, as Carlyle says, that our sorrow is the inverted image of our nobility, how deep must the sorrow have been of the noblest of our race! Well may the Greek liturgy, with infinite pathos, speak of His "unknown sorrows."

Shall the sufferings of Christ cause us to reject Christ? Ah, strange infatuation! As well reject the heaven because of its sun, or night because of the queenly moon, or a diadem because of its regal gem, or home because of mother.

The sufferings of Christ are the proudest boast of the Gospel. He himself wears the insignia of them in heaven; as a general, on the day of triumph, chooses his choicest order to wear upon his breast. Yes, and it was the deliberate choice of Him, "for Whom are all things, and by Whom are all things " - and Who must, therefore, have had every expedient at His command - that the path of suffering should be His Son's way through our world.

Every track through creation is as familiar to Omniscience as the tracks across the hills to the grey-haired, plaided shepherd. Had He wished, the Father might have conducted the Son to glory by another route than the thorny, flint-set path of suffering. But the reasons for this experience were so overwhelming that He could not evade them. Nothing else had been becoming. Those reasons may be stated almost in a sentence.

Our Father has on hand a work greater than his original creation. He is "bringing many sons unto glory." The way may be rugged and tedious, but its end is glory. And it is the way along which our Father is bringing us; for, since we believe on the Son, we have the right to call ourselves sons (John i. 12).

And there are many of us. Many sons, though only one Son. We do not go solitarily along the narrow way. We are but part of a multitude which no man can number. The glory of which we have already spoken, and into which Jesus has entered, is not for Him alone, but for us also. "Many sons" are to be His joint-heirs; reigning with Him on His throne, sharing His unsearchable riches and His everlasting reign.

But all these sons must tread the path of suffering. Since the first sin brought suffering to our first parents, and bloodshed into the first home, there has been but one lot for those who will live Godly. Their road leads to glory; but every inch of it is stained with their blood and watered by their tears. It climbs to Hermon's summit; but it descends immediately into sombre and devil-haunted plains. It conducts to the Mount of Olives, with its ascension light; but it first traverses the glades of Gethsemane, the wine-press of Golgotha, the solitude and darkness of the grave.

"The path of sorrow, and that path alone,
Leads to the land where sorrow is unknown."
What true soul has not its wilderness of temptation, its conflicts with Sadducees and Scribes, its hour of weariness and watching, its tears over cities full of rebellious men, its disappointments from friends, its persecutions from foes, rejection, agony, friendlessness, loneliness, denials, trial, treacheries, deaths, and burials? Such is the draught which the noblest and saintliest have drunk from the golden chalice of life.

Foreseeing our needs, our Father has provided for us a Leader It is a great boon for a company of pilgrims to have a Great-heart; for an army to have a captain; for an exodus to have a Moses. Courageous, sagacious, and strong leaders are God's good gifts to men. And it is only what we might have expected that God has placed such a One as the efficient Leader at the head of the long line of pilgrims, whom He is engaged in bringing to glory.

The toils seem lighter and the distance shorter; laggards quicken their pace; wandering ones are recalled from by-paths by the presence and voice of the Leader, who marches, efficient, royal, and divine, in the van. Oh heirs of glory, weary of the long and toilsome march, remember that you are part of a great host, and that the Prince, at the head of the column, has long since entered the city - though He is back again, passing as an inspiration along the ranks as they are toiling on.

Our Leader is perfect. Of course this does not refer to His moral or spiritual attributes. In these He is possessed of the stature of the perfect Man, and has filled out, in every detail, God's ideal of manhood. But He might have been all this without being perfectly adapted to the work of leading many sons through suffering to glory.

He might have been perfect in character, and desirous to help us, but, if He had never tasted death, how could he allay our fears as we tread the verge of Jordan? If He had never been tempted, how could He succour those who are tempted? If He had never wept, how could He staunch our tears? If He had never suffered, hungered, wearied on the hill of difficulty, or threaded His way through the quagmires of grief, how could He have been a merciful and faithful High-Priest, having compassion on the ignorant and wayward?

But, thank God, our Leader is a perfect one. He is perfectly adapted to His task. His certificate, countersigned by the voice of inspiration, declares Him fully qualified.

But this perfect efficiency, as we have seen, is the result of suffering. In no other conceivable way could He have been so effectively qualified to be our Leader as He has been by the ordeal of suffering. Every pang, every tear, every thrill, all were needed to complete His equipment to help us.

And from this we may infer that suffering is sometimes permitted to befall us in order to qualify us to be, in our poor measure, the leaders and comforters of our brethren, who are faltering in the march. When next we suffer, let us believe that it is not the result of chance, or fate, or man's carelessness, or Hell's malevolence, but that perhaps God is perfecting our adaptability to comfort and succour others.

Are there not some in your circle to whom you naturally betake yourself in times of trial and sorrow? They always seem to speak the right word, to give the very counsel you are longing for; you do not realise, however, the cost which they had to pay ere they became so skilful in binding up gaping wounds and drying tears.

But if you were to investigate their past history you would find that they have suffered more than most. They have watched the slow untwisting of some silver cord on which the lamp of life hung. They have seen the golden bowl of joy dashed to their feet, and its contents spilt. They have stood by ebbing tides, and drooping gourds, and noon sunsets; but all this has been necessary to make them the nurses, the physicians, the priests of men.

The boxes that come from foreign climes are clumsy enough, but they contain spices which scent the air with the fragrance of the Orient. So suffering is rough and hard to bear, but it hides beneath it discipline, education, possibilities, which not only leave us nobler, but perfect us to help others.

Do not fret, or set your teeth, or wait doggedly for the suffering to pass; but get out of it all you can, both for yourself and for your service to your generation, according to the will of God.

Suffering educates sympathy, it softens the spirit, lightens the touch, hushes the tread. It accustoms the spirit to read from afar the symptoms of an unspoken grief. It teaches the soul to tell the number of the promises, which, like the constellations of the arctic circle, shine most brilliantly through the wintry night. It gives to the spirit a depth, a delicacy, a wealth of which it cannot otherwise possess itself. Through suffering He has become perfected.

His sufferings have purchased our pardon. He tasted death for every man. But His sufferings have done more in enabling Him to understand experimentally, and to allay, with the tenderness of one who has suffered, all the griefs and sorrows that are experienced by the weakest and weariest of the great family of God.

So far, then, from rejecting Him because of His sorrows, this shall attract us the more quickly to His side. And, amid our glad songs, this note shall predominate: "It behoved Christ to suffer." "In the midst of the throne, a Lamb as it had been slain."

CHAPTER 7: THE DEATH OF DEATH

"Forasmuch then as the children are partakers of flesh and blood, He also himself likewise took part of the same; that through death He might destroy him that had the power of death, that is, the Devil; and deliver them, who through fear of death were all their lifetime subject to bondage." (HEBREWS 2.14-15).

WE fear death with a double fear. There is, first, the instinctive fear shared also by the animal creation, for the very brutes tremble as the moment of death draws near. Surely this fear is not wrong. It is often congenital and involuntary, and afflicts some of God's noblest saints, though doubtless these will some day confess that it was most unwarrantable, and that the moment of dissolution was calm and sweet and blessed.

It is a growing opinion among thoughtful men that the moment of death, when the spirit passes from its earthly tabernacle, is probably the most painless and the happiest moment of its whole earthly story. And if this be so generally, how much more must it be the case with those on whose sight are breaking the glories of Paradise!

The child whose eyes feast upon a glowing vista of flower and fruit, beckoning it through the garden gate, hardly notices the rough woodwork of the gate itself as it bounds through; and probably the soul, becoming aware of the beauty of the King and the glories of its home, is too absorbed to notice the act of death, till it suddenly finds itself free to mount and soar and revel in the dawning light.

But there is another fear of death, which is spiritual dread at its mystery. What is it? Whither does it lead? Why does it come just now? What is the nature of the life beyond? We see the movements on the other side of the thick curtain which sways to and fro, but we can distinguish no form. The dying ones are conscious of sights and sounds for which we strain eye and ear in vain.

We dread its leave-taking. The heathen poet sang sadly of leaving earth and home and family. Long habit endears the homeliest lot and the roughest comrades. How much more the true-hearted and congenial - it is hard to part from them. If only we could all go together, there would be nothing in it. But this separate dropping-off, this departing one by one, this drift from the anchorage alone! Who can deny that it is a lonesome thing?

Men dread what lies after death. "The sting of death is sin." The sinner dreads to die, because he knows that, on the other side of death, he must meet the God against whom he has sinned, and stand at His bar to give an account and receive the due reward of His deeds. How can he face that burning glory? How can he answer for one of a thousand? How can mortal man be just with God? How can he escape Hell, and find his place amid the happy festal throngs of the Golden City?

Many of man's fears were known to Christ. And He knew that they would be felt by many who were to be closely related to Him as brethren. If, then, He was prompted by ordinary feelings of compassion to the great masses of mankind, He would be especially moved to relieve those with whom he had so close an affinity, as these marvellous verses unfold.

He and they are all of one (verse 11). He calls them brethren through the lips of psalmist and prophet (verse 12). He takes His stand in the assembled Church, and sings His Father's praise in its company (verse I 2). He even associates Himself with them in their humble childlike trust (verse 13).

He dares to accost the gaze of all worlds, as He comes forward leading them by the hand (verse 13). Oh, marvellous identification! Oh, rapturous association! More wondrous far than if a seraph should cherish friendship with a worm! But the preciousness of this relationship lies in the fact that Jesus will do all He can to alleviate that fear of death, which is more or less common to us all.

But in order to do it, He must die. He could not be the death of death unless He had personally tasted death. He needed to fulfil the law of death by dying, before He could abolish death. Our David must go into the valley of Elah, and grapple with our giant foe, and wrest from him his power, and slay him with his own sword.

As in the old fable Prometheus could not slay the Minotaur unless he accompanied the yearly freight of victims, so must Jesus go with the myriads of our race into the dark confines of the tomb, that death might do its worst in vain; that the grave might lose its victory; and that the grim gaoler might be shown powerless to hold the Resurrection and the Life.

Had Christ not died, it might have been affirmed that, in one place at least, death and sin, chaos and darkness, were supreme. "It behoved Him, therefore, to suffer, and to rise from the dead the third day." (Luke 24.46) And, like another Samson, carrying the gates of his prison-house, He came forth, demonstrating forever that light is stronger than darkness, salvation than sin, life than death.

Hear His triumphant cry, as thrice the risen and ascended Master exclaims, "I died, and lo, I am alive forevermore, and have the keys of Hades and of death." (Revelation 1.18). Death and hell chose their own battleground, their strongest; and there, in the hour of His weakness, our King defeated them, and now carries the trophy of victory at His girdle forevermore. Hallelujah!

But He could only have died by becoming man. Perhaps there is no race in the universe that can die but our own. So there may be no other spot in the wide universe of God seamed with graves, shadowed by the outspread wings of the angel of death, or marked by the plague-spot of sin.

"Sin entered into the world, and death by sin; and so death passed upon all" (Romans 5.12). In order then to die, Christ must take on Himself our human nature. Others die because they are born; Christ was born that He might die.

It is as if He said: "Of you, Oh human mother, must I be born; and I must suffer the aches and pains and sorrows of mortal life; and I must hasten quickly to the destined goal of human life; I have come into the world to die."

"Forasmuch as the children are partakers of flesh and blood, He also Himself likewise took part of the same, in order that through death He might destroy Him that had the power of death, that is, the Devil, and deliver them, who through fear of death were all their lifetime subject to bondage."

BY DEATH CHRIST DESTROYED HIM THAT HAD THE POWER OF DEATH.

Scripture has no doubt as to the existence of the Devil. And those who know much of their own inner life, and of the sudden assaults of evil to which we are liable, cannot but realise his terrible power. And from this passage we infer that that power was even greater before Jesus died.

"He had the power of death." It was a chief weapon in his infernal armoury. The dread of it was so great as to drive men to yield to any demands made by the priests of false religions, with their dark impurities and hideous rites. Thus timid sheep are scared by horrid shouts and blows into the butcher's shambles.

But since Jesus died, the devil and his power are destroyed. Brought to naught, not made extinct. Still he assails the Christian warrior, though armed from head to foot; and goes about seeking whom he may devour, and deceives men to ruin. Satan is not impotent though chained. He has received the wound which annuls his power, but it has not yet been effectual to destroy him.

His power was broken at the cross and grave of Jesus. The hour of Gethsemane was the hour and power of darkness. And Satan must have seen the Resurrection in despair. It was the knell of his destiny. It sealed his doom. The prince of this world was judged and cast out from the seat of power (John 12.31; 16.11). The serpent's head was bruised beyond remedy.

Fear not the Devil, 0 child of God, nor death! These make much noise, but they have no power. The Breaker has gone before you, clearing your way. Only keep close behind Him. Hark ! He gives you power over all the power of the enemy, and nothing shall by any means hurt you (Luke 10.9). No robber will pluck you from your Shepherd's hand.

BY DEATH CHRIST DELIVERS FROM THE FEAR OF DEATH.

A child was in the habit of playing in a large and beautiful garden, with sunny lawns; but there was one part of it, a long and winding path, down which he never ventured. Indeed, he dreaded to go near it, because some silly nurse had told him that ogres and goblins dwelt within its darksome gloom. At last his eldest brother heard of his fear, and, after playing one day with him, took him to the embowered entrance of the grove, and, leaving him there terror-stricken, went singing through its length, and returned, and reasoned with the child, proving that his fears were groundless.

At last he took the lad's hand, and they went through it together, and from that moment the fear which had haunted the place fled. And the memory of that brother's presence took its place. So has Jesus done for us!

Fear not the mystery Of death! Jesus has died and shown us that it is the gateway into another life, more fair and blessed than this life in which human words are understood, and human faces smile, and human affections linger still. The forty days of His resurrection life have solved many of the problems, and illumined most of the mystery.

To die is to go at once to be with Him. No chasm, no interval, no weary delay in purgatory. Absent from the body, present with the Lord, One moment here in conditions of mortality; the next beyond the stars.

Fear not the loneliness of death! The soul in the dark valley becomes aware of another at its side, "You are with me." Death cannot separate us, even for a moment, from the love of God, which is in Christ Jesus our Lord. In the hour of death Jesus fulfils His own promise, "I will come again and take you unto myself." (John 14.3). And on the other side we step into a vast circle of loving spirits, who welcome the newcomer with festal songs (2 Peter 1.11).

Fear not the after-death! The curse and penalty of sin have been borne by Him. Death, the supreme sentence on sinners, has been suffered for us by our Substitute. In Him we have indeed passed on to the other side of the doom which is justly ours as members of a sinful race. Who is he that condemns? It is Christ that died, yes, rather, that is risen again." (Romans 8.34).

Death! How shall they die who have already died in Christ? That which others call death we call sleep. We dread it no more than sleep. Our bodies lie down exhausted with the long working day, to awake in the fresh energy of the eternal morning, but in the meanwhile the spirit is presented faultless before the presence of His glory with exceeding joy.

CHAPTER 8: CHRIST'S MERCIFUL AND FAITHFUL HELP

"We have a merciful and faithful high-priest in things pertaining to God." (HEBREWS 2.17).

DO you wonder that your Lord was tempted and sorrowful? It is indeed the marvel of eternity, and yet not so marvellous, when we consider the beings whom He elected to succour, help, and save, and of whom each of us is one.

Had He chosen to lay hold of fallen angels, with a view of raising them from their lost estate, He would without doubt have taken upon Himself their nature, and descended into the pit; identifying Himself with their miseries, and paving, by His sufferings, a pathway across the great fixed gulf which intervenes between their lost estate and Paradise.

But verily He took not hold of angels, but of the seed of Abraham, and had no alternative therefore but to assimilate Himself in all points to the nature of those whom, in infinite mercy and grace, He brothered.

There are two things you need, reader; and not you only, but all men, reconciliation, and succour in the hour of temptation. These instinctive cravings of the soul are as mighty and as irrepressible as the craving of the body for sleep or food, and they are as evident amid our luxury and refinement as in primeval forests, or beside the historic rivers of antiquity - the Nile, the Indus, the Euphrates.

To meet these two needs, men have constituted one of their number a priest. That word has an ominous sound to our ears, because it has been associated with immoralities and cruelty. The world has never seen more unscrupulous or rapacious tyrants than its priests, whether of Baal or Moloch, of Judaism or the Papacy.

All through the ages it has seemed impossible for men to receive power in the spiritual realm without abusing it to the injury of those who sought their help.

Study the history of the priesthood, which murdered Christ because He threw too strong a light upon its hypocrisies and villainies, and you have the history of every priestcraft which has darkened the world with crime, and saturated its soil with the blood of the noblest and saintliest of men.

And yet the idea of the priest is a natural and a beautiful one. It is natural for men who are conscious of sin barring their access into the presence of a holy God, and demanding sacrifice in order to make peace, to say to one of their fellows, "Our hands are stained with blood, and grimed with toil, our garments spotted with pollution and dust, our lives too busy for us to spare time for those rites which alone can fit the sinner to stand before the eye of God. Do for us what we cannot do for ourselves, prepare yourself by holy rite and vigil and fasting from sin, so as to be able to stand in the presence-chamber of the All-Holy; and when you have acquired the right of audience with Him, speak for us, atone for us, make reconciliation for our sins; and then come forth to us, succouring and blessing those who cannot attain to your position, but must ever struggle as best they may with the strong, rough, bad world in which they are doomed to live."

This seems the underlying thought behind the vast system which has built temples in every land, reared altars on every soil, and constituted a priesthood amid the most degraded as well as the most civilised races of mankind.

And there is great beauty in the work and ministry of a true priest. Not always engaged in the darker work of sacrificing flocks of fleecy sheep, by which alone, in those rude days, the cost of sin could be computed; the true priest would have other, and, perhaps, more congenial work.

He would be the shepherd of the timid souls around him, listening to confessions whispered over the heads of the dumb victims, feeling compassion for erring and wayward ones, comforting those who were passing through scenes of sorrow, till faces shadowed with tears began to gleam with holy light; arresting the proud hand of the oppressor, as Ambrose did in lawless days, to rescue the poor from the mailed blow. Never studying self-interest, never consulting ease or pleasure or gain, never resting while one poor wanderer was away in the snowdrift or on the wild.

Yes, and more, he would be the spokesman of souls, praying for those who did not pray for themselves, praying for those who knew not what or how to ask, interceding for the whole race of man. Ah! how often must such a one have been compelled by the pressure of the burden to go apart from the busy crowds to some lone spot, that he might pour out before God the long litany of need and sorrow and temptation which had been poured into his heart. Lovely ideal, ah, how seldom realised!

All this is Jesus Christ, and more. Words fail indeed to say all that He is in Himself, or all that He can be to those that trust Him. And it is because of this that He is able to give such blessed help to all who need it. Let us consider that help.

IT IS SOVEREIGN AND UNEXPECTED HELP.

Angels fell. Once they were the peers of heaven. They sang its songs, plucked its flowers of amaranth, and drank its tranquil bliss. They loved its King, and served Him, like the sunbeam, with unpolluted brightness and unswerving direction. But, alas! they fell from heaven to hell. And for them there is no help, so far as we can learn. "God takes not hold of angels."

But He has set His heart upon us, the poor children of dust, the creatures of the transient moments of time, who had fallen by the same sin of self-will. Here is a theme for meditation! We cannot pierce the mystery, or understand its full import. But we may, with wondering faith and joy, accept the chalice, brimming with unmerited, unexpected, undeserved grace, and drain its draughts of bliss.

IT IS HUMAN HELP.

" Made like to his brethren." The peculiarity of this phrase testifies to Christ's pre-existence and glory, and indicates how great a stoop on His part it involved ere he could be like man. He had to be made like man, He was not like man in the original constitution of His being.

We cannot solve the mystery of the holy incarnation. And yet the thought of it has never been quite foreign to the heart of man. Many a Greek and Hindu myth rested on an instinctive craving for the presence of God in human flesh, which became parent to the belief that such a thing had been, and might be again. Even in the highlands of Galatia, the most ready explanation of the miracles of Paul was that the gods had come down in the likeness of men.

But though there be such a profound mystery resting on this subject, yet the union of the Almighty with a human life is at least not more incomprehensible than the union of a spiritual, unmaterial principle, as the soul, with a material organism, as the human body. When the secrets of our own nature have been unravelled, it will be time enough for us to demand of the Almighty that, when He assumes our nature, He should disrobe Himself of all mystery.

How exquisite is the arrangement that God's help should come to us through the Son of Man; that our Helper should shed true human tears, and feel true human pity, Jew though he was, child of the most exclusive and intolerant of peoples, yet the humanity which is greater than Judaism makes us oblivious to all else than that He is our Brother.

IT IS HIGH-PRIESTLY HELP.

The full meaning of this phrase will appear as we proceed. It is sufficient to say here, that all that men have sought to realise in human priesthoods, but in vain, is realised with transcendent beauty in Him. Nor is there any way of weaning men from the human priesthoods which deceive, but to present to them the all-glorious, immaculate priesthood of Christ.

It is of little use only to denounce the priests that are coming back to Protestant England through a thousand covert channels, or the people who go to them. There is a craving in their heart which impels them. It is of no use to fight against nature.

But satisfy it, give it its true nutriment; supply its wants with reality, and it will be content to drop the false for the true, the paste diamond for the Golconda pebbles, the human for the divine.

Men must have a priest; and they are going back to the mummeries of Rome, because there has been too scanty a presentation in our pulpits of the priesthood of Jesus.

IT IS MERCIFUL AND FAITHFUL HELP.

When we are in need, we want help wedded with mercy. The patient in the infirmary does not like to be treated as a broken watch. Oh that he were at home again, to be nursed by the soft hands of his mother, which ever feel so skilful and gentle and soft! We need merciful help, which does not upbraid, is not in too great a hurry to listen, and gladly takes all extenuating circumstances into account. Such mercy is in the heart of Jesus.

And His help is ever faithful, too. This word has a fine tint of meaning, almost lost in our translation, giving the idea of one who runs up at the first cry of distress. He neither slumbers nor sleeps. He watches us with a gaze which is not for a moment diverted from us. He sees us through the storm. He sits beside the molten metal. He will help us right early i.e. when the day breaks.

You may be bereft of all power of consecutive thought, unable to utter a single intelligible sentence, frantic with agony and remorse, but if you can only moan, He will instantly respond. "He will be very gracious to you at the voice of your cry."

IT IS HELP BASED ON RECONCILIATION FOR SIN.

Sin is one of the greatest facts in our history. It is impossible to ignore it. You cannot explain man unless you take it into account. For this the world has been covered with the apparatus of sacrifice; and the cry has rung in a monotone of despair, "How shall man be just with God?"

But Jesus met the demands of conscience, echoing those of a broken law, when on Calvary, as High-Priest, He offered himself as victim, and made an all-sufficient, satisfactory, and complete sacrifice for the sin of the world.

Burdened one, groaning under the load of sin, remember that He bore your sins in His own body on the tree. Approach the holy God, reminding Him of that fact, and daring on account of it to stand unabashed and accepted in His sight.

IT IS SYMPATHETIC HELP FOR THE TEMPTED.

" Them that are tempted." Within that circle we all stand. Each is tempted in subtler, if not in grosser, forms, in extraordinary, if not in ordinary, ways. You have been trying, oh, so hard, to be good, but have met with some sudden gust, and been overcome.

Tempted to despair! Tempted to yield to Potiphar's wife! Tempted to become a brute! No dawn without the fowler's snare! No day without its sorrow! No night without its noisome pestilence! No rose without its thorn!

Do we not need succour? Certainly; and He is able to succour the tempted, because He has suffered the very worst that temptation can do. Not that there was ever one symptom or thought of yielding, yet suffering to the point of extreme anguish, beneath the test.

Oh sufferers, tempted ones, desolate and not comforted, lean your heads against the breast of the God-Man, Whose feet have trodden each inch of your thorny path, and Whose experiences of the power of evil well qualify Him to strengthen you to stand, to lift you up if you have fallen, to speak such words as will heal the ache of the freshly gaping wound. If He were impassive, and had never wept or fought in the Garden shadows, or cried out forsaken on the cross, we had not felt Him so near as we can do now in all hours of bitter grief.

Oh matchless Saviour, on Whom God our Father has laid our help, we can dispense with human sympathy, with priestly help, with the solace and stay of many a holy service; but You are indispensable to us, in Your life, and death, and resurrection, and brotherhood, and sympathising intercession at the throne of God!

CHAPTER 9: A WARNING AGAINST UNBELIEF

"Take heed, brethren, lest there be in any of you an evil heart of unbelief, in departing from the living God." - HEBREWS 3.12.

THE contrast between the third and fourth chapters of this epistle is very marked. The former is like a drear November day, when all the landscape is drenched by sweeping rain, and the rotting leaves fall in showers to find a grave upon the damp and muddy soil. The latter is like a still clear day in midsummer, when nature revels in reposeful bliss beneath the unstinted caresses of the sun. There is as much difference between them as between the seventh and eighth chapters of the Epistle to the Romans.

But each chapter represents an experience of the inner Christian life. Perhaps the majority of Christians live and die in the third chapter, to their infinite loss. Comparatively few pass over into the fourth.

Yet why, reader, should you not pass the boundary line today, and leave behind forever the bitter, unsatisfactory experiences which have become the normal rule of your existence? Come up out of the wilderness, in which you have wandered so long. Your sojourn there has been due, not to any desire on the part of God, or to any arbitrary appointment of His, or to any natural disability of your temperament; but to certain grave failures on your part, in the regimen of the inner life.

The antipodes of your hitherto dreary experiences is Christ, the unsearchable riches of Christ, to be made a partaker of Christ. For Christ is the Promised Land that flows with milk and honey, in which we eat bread without scarceness, and gather the grapes and pomegranates and olives of rare spiritual blessedness.

WILDERNESS EXPERIENCES. Never did a nation occupy a prouder position than the children of Israel on the morning when they stood victorious on the shores of the Red Sea. The power of the tyrant had been broken by a series of marvellous miracles. The chivalry of Egypt had sunk as lead in the mighty waters of death.

And as the sun rose behind the mountains of Edom, and struck a flashing pathway across the burnished mirror of the sea, it revealed long lines of corpses washed up to the water's edge. Behind, Egypt left forever. Above, the fleecy cloud, chariot of God, tabernacle for His presence. Before, the Land of Promise.

Many a man was already dreaming of vineyards and olive yards, and a settled home, all of which lay within two or three months' easy march.

But of those six hundred thousand men, flushed with victory and hope, two only were destined to see the land flowing with milk and honey; and these not until forty weary years had slowly passed away.

And what became of all the rest? Alas! their carcasses fell in the wilderness. Instead of reposing in some family burying-place in the Land of Promise, their bodies were taken up one by one and laid in the desert waste, the sands their winding-sheet, the solitude their mausoleum.

It took forty years for them all to die. And to accomplish this there must have been a high percentage of deaths. How dreary those incessant funerals! How monotonous the perpetual sounds of Oriental grief moaning through the camp! What wonder that Psalm 90, written among such scenes, is so inexpressibly sad!

The wilderness experience is emblematic, amongst other things, of unrest, aimlessness, and unsatisfied longings.

Unrest. The tents were constantly being struck to be erected again in much the same spot. Theirs a perpetual weariness, and they were not suffered to enter into God's rest.

Aimlessness. They wandered in the wilderness in a desert way; they found no city of habitation.

Unsatisfied longings. Hungry and thirsty, their soul fainted in them.

But how typical of the lives of many amongst ourselves! Life is passing away so swiftly from us, but how unideal! How few Christians seem to have learned the secret of the inner rest! How many are the victims of murmuring and discontent, or are bitten by the serpents of jealousy and passion, of hatred and ill-will!

The almost universal experience tells of broken vows and blighted hopes, of purposeless wanderings, of a monotony of failure. Always striking and pitching the camp! Always surrounded by the same monotonous horizon, sand, with here and there a palm tree! Always fed on the same food, till the soul loathes it! Life passes away amid fret and chafing disappointment and weariness of existence, till we say with Solomon, "Vanity of vanities, all is vanity."

One of the scourges of the desert is the sandstorm, when the hot wind is laden with light powdery dust, which finds its way into eyes and mouth and lungs, penetrating the clothes, stinging the skin, and making life almost unbearable. An apt illustration of the small annoyances, the petty irritations, the perpetual swarm of gnat-like stings, which invade our most comfortable circumstances, and make us question whether life is worth living.

Then there is also the mirage. When from afar green glades seem to attract the weary traveller, who, as he reaches them, finds his hopes deceived and his thirst mocked. Emblem this of the disappointments to which they expose themselves who are ever seeking for some earthly good to mitigate the hardships and sorrows of their life, instead of seeking the fellowship and blessed help of the living Christ. They travel forward, thinking at every step that they are nearing an oasis in their desert march; but, as they approach, the fabric of their hopes fades away into the air.

"We are made partakers of Christ." These words may either mean that all believers together partake of the fullness of Jesus, or that they all partake with Him of the fullness of God. "Heirs of God, and joint-heirs with Christ."

But whichever be the true rendering, the thought is inexpressibly helpful. Jesus Christ is our Promised Land, and our Joshua to lead us thither. He gives us rest. In Him are orchards and vineyards, and all manner of precious things. His comfort for our sorrow; His rest for our weariness, His strength for our weakness, His purity for our corruption, His ever-present help for our need. Oh, blessed Jesus, surely it is the wonder of heaven that we make so little of You!

THE CAUSE OF THE WILDERNESS EXPERIENCE.

They could not enter in because of unbelief. See how unbelief raises a barrier which shuts us out of blessing. A fortune may have been left you, but if you do not believe the intelligence and apply for it, you will not profit by it. A regiment of angels may be passing by your home, with blessings in their hands that might enrich you forever, but if you do not believe the tidings that they are on the march, you will not go out to greet or welcome them.

A noble character may rear itself in the neighbourhood in which you live, or the society in which you move; but if you do not believe in it, you will derive no stimulus or comfort from its genial and helpful influence. So whatever Christ may be, and however near, He will be nothing to you unless you have learned to trust Him.

There are three conditions in which unbelief thrives with us, as with the children of Israel.

1) "They murmured".

The first outbreak was in the wilderness of Sin (Exodus 16), within a few days of the Exodus. There was no bread. The provisions hastily brought from Egypt were consumed. They had their kneading-troughs, but no flour to knead. There was no organised commissariat.

"And the whole congregation of the children of Israel murmured against Moses and against Aaron in the wilderness, and the children of Israel said unto them, Would that we had died by the hand of the Lord in the land of Egypt, when we sat by the flesh-pots, when we did eat bread to the full, for you have brought us forth into this wilderness, to kill this whole assembly with hunger."

The second outbreak was at Rephidim (Exodus 17). There was no water. The scanty desert brooks were heaps of scorching stones, and not a leaf of vegetation trembled in the burning sunshine. And again the sullen sounds of discontent were heard as the people muttered their belief that they had been brought out of Egypt to perish there.

But the most serious outbreak occurred shortly after they left Sinai (Numbers 13). The green hills of Palestine at last appeared in view, and spies were sent forward to search the land. After forty days they returned laden with luscious fruits; but they had a story to tell of the strength and fortifications of the Canaanites, which filled the people with dismay; and "all the people murmured against Moses and against Aaron, and said, Would God that we had died in the land of Egypt."

"Yes, they despised the pleasant land, they believed not His word, but murmured in their tents, and hearkened not to the voice of the Lord. Therefore He lifted up His hand to them, that He would overthrow them in the wilderness" (Psalm 106.24-26).

A murmuring, complaining heart is one which has already commenced to disbelieve in the wise and loving lead of Christ, and in which unbelief will thrive.

2). "They departed from the living God." God is the Home and Source of life. From Him, as from a fountain, all things derive their being, strength, and beauty. If Israel had remained in living union with Him, there would have been no failure in their supplies, and there would have been sufficient grace to make the people calm and restful and strong amid these privations and difficulties.

But they departed from Him. They thought they could do better for themselves. They forsook the Fountain of living water, and went up into the hills to hew out for themselves broken, i.e. cracked cisterns, which could hold no water.

Of the Rock that begat them they grew unmindful; and so became as the desert tamarisk, which inhabits dull and uninhabited wastes, in contrast to the tree whose roots are fed by rivers, and whose arms shadow generations.

Let us ask ourselves whether there has been any declension in our heart-religion, less prayerfulness, less closeness in our walk with God, less enjoyment in the worship of His house; for, if so, unbelief is sure to manifest itself, as the fungus which grows fat on the damp and fetid soil. Unbelief cannot live in the sunlight of fellowship with God.

3). They failed to learn the lessons of the past. They did not deny the past. They would have told you with flashing eyes the wonderful story of deliverance. But they did not trust God's love and wisdom, they did not rely on His repeated promises that He would most certainly bring them in as He had already brought them out; they did not find in the past a guarantee that He would not fail nor forsake them.

At Sin they should have said, "He gave us these bodies with these appetites and needs: we may trust Him to provide them with food. 'Our heavenly Father knows that we have need of all these things'."

At Marah they should have said, "He gave us manna, surely He can supply our thirst."

At Paran they should have said, "God has promised to give us the land; and so, though the Canaanites are strong, and their cities walled to heaven, we will dare believe in Him." Instead of this they cried, "He smote the rock, and the waters gushed out; and the streams overflowed. Can He give bread also? Can He give flesh for his people?"

As we pass through life we should carefully store our hearts with the memory of God's great goodness, and fetch from past deliverances the assurances that He will never leave, neither forsake.

Has He conveyed us across the Atlantic to leave us to drown in a ditch? Has He been with us in six troubles to desert us in the seventh? Has He saved, and can he not keep? Has He redeemed us from hell, and can He not bring us to heaven?

"His love in time past forbids us to think
He'll leave us at last in trouble to sink;
Each sweet Ebenezer we have in review
Confirms His good pleasure to help us right through."

If we would guard against unbelief, we should reinforce our faith by constantly recapitulating the story of God's past dealings, and thus, through the stream of memory, the uplands of our life will send their deposits of blessed helpfulness to reinforce us in our daily anxieties and perplexities. "The Lord has been mindful of us, He will bless us." "If, when we were enemies, we were reconciled to God by the death of His Son, much more, being reconciled, we shall be saved by His life."

You were happy in your childhood. Your early days were set in a golden frame. But dear ones have vanished, as the oak's shadow from the forest undergrowth, and you feel unprotected and lonely. But the God of your childhood will not be less thoughtful of you than in those happy bygone days.

You have stepped out on the waters, and as the storm threatens you, you almost wish yourself back, but He who was with you in the fair haven will be as near you when the winds rave and the waves lift up their voice.

You are on the point of exchanging the flesh-pots of Egypt for the new land of Canaan, with its blessed promise, and on the way, heart and flesh fail at the new and untried scenes that daunt and perplex. But He who delivered you from Pharaoh can shield you from Amalek; He who cleft the Red Sea will divide the Jordan.

INSPIRED CAUTIONS. " Take heed lest there be in any one of you an evil heart of unbelief in departing from the living God."

Unbelief is the child, not of the head, but of the heart. It is always well to know the source of disease, then the physician can attack it in its citadel. If unbelief were the creature of our intellect, we must needs meet it there with argument, but since it is the product of a wrong state of heart, of an evil heart, we must meet it there.

"This," says William Law, "is an eternal truth, which you cannot too much reflect upon, that reason always follows the state of the heart; and what your heart is, that is your reason. If your heart is full of sentiments, of penitence, and of faith, your reason will take part with your heart; but if your heart is shut up in death and dryness, your reason will delight in nothing but dry objections and speculations."

Guard against an evil heart. If the heart were in a right condition, faith would be as natural to it as flowers in spring, or as smiles on the face of healthy, innocent childhood. As soon as the heart gets into an evil state - harbouring sin, cherishing things which you would not excuse in others but condone in yourself, permitting unholy thoughts and desires to remain unchecked and unjudged, then, beware! for such a heart is no longer able to believe in God. Its head turns dizzy, its eyes are blinded, and it is in imminent peril of falling irretrievably.

Take heed, then. Watch and pray. Examine yourselves whether you be in the faith. Prove your own selves! Expose yourselves to the searching light of God's Spirit. Cultivate the honest and good heart.

Most of the infidelity of the present day arises from man's disinclination to retain God in his knowledge. More scepticism may be traced to a neglected prayer closet than to the arguments of infidels or the halls of secularists.

First men depart from God, then they deny Him. And, therefore, for the most part, unbelief will not yield to clever sermons on the evidences, but to home thrusts that pierce the points of the harness to the soul within. "Keep your heart beyond all keeping, since out of it are the issues of life."

Guard especially against heart-hardening. Hard hearts are unbelieving ones, therefore beware of ossification of the heart. The hardest hearts were soft once, and the softest may get hard. The chalk which now holds the fossil shells was once moist ooze. The horny hand of toil was once full of soft dimples. The murderer once shuddered when, as a boy, he crushed a worm. Judas must have been once a tender and impressionable lad.

But hearts harden gradually, like the freezing of a pond on a frosty night. At first the process can be detected by none but a practised eye. Then there is a thin film of ice, so slender that a pin or needle would fall through. At length it will sustain a pebble, and, if winter still hold its unbroken sway, a child, a man, a crowd, a cart will follow. We get hard through the steps of an unperceived process.

The constant hearing the truth without obeying it. The knowing a better and doing the worse. The cherishing of unholy things that seem fair as angels. The refusal to confess the wrong and to profess the right. All these things harden. Beware of the deceitfulness of sin! Take heed to yourselves! Exhort one another daily.

Guard against a fickle heart. This is the sin which this epistle especially opposes. There are many around us who eagerly embrace a novelty, but when the stress comes, as it always does, like the settling of a house, there is a slackening off. We must hold fast our boldness and the glorying of our hope steadfast to the end. We can only become partakers of Christ if we hold fast the beginning of our confidence firm to the end.

We should see not only to our own heart, but to the heart of our brethren; and exhort one another daily, watching over each other, and seeking to revive drooping piety and reanimate fainting hope.

Let us take heed to these things today. Now is God's time. The Holy Ghost says, 'Today'. Every day of delay is dangerous, because the hardening process becomes more habitual.

Today restore what you have taken wrongfully, adjust a wrong, promote a right. Today renounce some evil habit, some unhallowed pastime, some unlawful friendship. Today reach out after some further realisation of the fair ideal which beckons you. Today leave the wilderness forever, and enter by faith the Land of Promise.

CHAPTER 10: THE GOSPEL OF REST

"There remains therefore a rest to the people of God." - (HEBREWS 4.9)

THE keynote of this chapter is Rest. In the second verse it is spoken of as a gospel, or good news. And is there any gospel that more needs preaching in these busy, weary days, through which our age is rushing to its close, than the Gospel of Rest?

On all hands we hear of strong and useful workers stricken down in early life by the exhausting effects of mental toil. The tender brain tissues were never made to sustain the tremendous wear and tear of our times. There is no machinery in human nature to repair swiftly enough the waste of nervous energy which is continually going on. It is not, therefore, to be wondered at that the symptoms of brain tiredness are becoming familiar to many workers, acting as warning signals, which, if not immediately attended to, are followed by some terrible collapse of mind or body, or both.

And yet it is not altogether that we work so much harder than our forefathers, but that there is so much more fret and chafe and worry in our lives. Competition is closer. Population is more crowded. Brains are keener and swifter in their motion. The resources of ingenuity and inventiveness, of creation and production, are more severely and constantly taxed. And the age seems so merciless and selfish.

If the lonely spirit trips and falls, it is trodden down in the great onward rush, or left behind to its fate, and the dread of the swoop of the vultures, with rustling wings, from unknown heights upon us as their prey, fills us with an anguish which we know by the familiar name of care.

We could better stand the strain of work if only we had rest from worry, from anxiety, and from the fret of the troubled sea that cannot rest, as it moans around us, with its yeasty waves, hungry to devour. Is such a rest possible?

This chapter states that such a rest is possible. "Let us labour therefore to enter into that rest." Rest? What rest? His rest, says the first verse, my rest, says the third verse, God's rest, says the fourth verse. And this last verse is a quotation from the earliest page of the Bible, which tells how God rested from all the work that He had made.

And as we turn to that marvellous apocalypse of the past, which in so many respects answers to the apocalypse of the future given us by the Apostle John, we find that, whereas we are expressly told of the evening and morning of each of the other days of creation, there is no reference to the dawn or close of God's rest-day, and we are left to infer that it is impervious to time, independent of duration, unlimited, and eternal, that the ages of human story are but hours in the rest-day of Yahweh, and that, in point of fact, we spend our years in the Sabbath-keeping of God.

But, better than all, it would appear that we are invited to enter into it and share it, as a child living by the placid waters of a vast fresh water lake may dip into them its cup, and drink and drink again, without making any appreciable diminution of its volume or ripple on its expanse.

What is meant by God resting? Surely not the rest of weariness! "He faints not, neither is weary." Though He had spread forth the heavens, and laid the foundations of the earth, and weighed the mountains in scales, and the hills in a balance, and had invented ten thousand differing forms of being, yet His inventiveness was as fresh, His energy as vigorous as ever.

Surely not the rest of inactivity. "My Father works hitherto," said our Lord. "In Him we live, and move, and have our being." True, He is not now sending forth, so far as we know, suns, or systems, or fresh types of being. But His power is ever at work, repairing, renewing, and sustaining the fabric of the vast machinery of the universe. No sparrow falls to the ground without Him. The cry of the young lion and the lowing of the oxen in the pastures attract His instant regard.

"In Him all things consist." It was the rest of a finished work. He girded Himself to the specific work of creation, and summoned into being all that is, and when it was finished He said it was very good, and at once He rested from all His work which He had created and made.

It was the rest of divine complacency, of infinite satisfaction, of perfect content. It was equivalent to saying, "This creation of Mine is all that I meant it to be, finished and perfect. I am perfectly satisfied. There is nothing more to be done. It is all very good."

This, then, is the rest which we are invited to share. We are not summoned to the heavy slumber which follows over-taxing toil, nor to inaction or indolence, but to the rest which is possible amid swift activity and strenuous work, to perfect equilibrium between the outgoings and incomings of the life, to a contented heart, to peace that passes all understanding, to the repose of the will in the will of God, and to the calm of the depths of the nature which are undisturbed by the hurricanes which sweep the surface, and urge forward the mighty waves.

This rest is holding out both its hands to the weary souls of men throughout the ages, offering its shelter as a harbour from the storms of life.

But is it certain that this rest has not already been entered and exhausted by the children of men? That question is fully examined and answered in this wonderful paragraph.

The Sabbath did not realise that rest (verse 3). We cannot prize its ministry too highly. Its law is written, not only in Scripture, but in the nature of man. The godless band of French Revolutionists found that they could not supersede the week by the decade, the one-day-in-seven by the one-day-in-ten. Like a ministering angel it relieves the monotony of labour, and hushes the ponderous machinery of life, and weaves its spell of rest, but it is too fitful and transient to realise the rest of God.

It may typify it, but it cannot exhaust it. Indeed, it was broken by man's rebellion as soon as God had sanctified and hallowed it. Canaan did not realise that rest (verse 8). The Land of Promise was a great relief to the marchings and privations of the desert. But it was constantly interrupted, and at last, in the Captivity, broken up, as the forms of the mountains in the lake by a shower of hail.

Besides, in the Book of Psalms, written four hundred years after Joshua had led Israel across the Jordan, The Holy Spirit, speaking by David, points onward to a rest still future (Psalm95.7).

Surely, then, if neither of these events has realised the rest of God, it remains still, waiting for us and all the people of God. "There remains, therefore," unexhausted and unrealised, "a Sabbath-keeping to the people of God."

And there is yet a further reason for this conviction of God's unexhausted rest. Jesus, our Forerunner and Representative, has entered into it for us. See what verse 10 affirms: "He that is entered into his rest; " and who can he be but our great Joshua, Jehovah-Jesus? He also has ceased from His own work of redemption, as God did from His of creation. After the creative act, there came the Sabbath, when God ceased from His work, and pronounced it very good. So, after the redemptive act, there came the Sabbath to the Redeemer.

He lay, during the seventh day, in the grave of Joseph, not because He was exhausted or inactive, but because redemption was finished, and there was no more for Him to do. He sat down at the right hand of the Majesty on High, and that majestic session is a symptom neither of fatigue nor of indolence.

He ever lives to make intercession; He works with His servants, confirming their words with signs; He walks amid the seven golden candlesticks. And yet He rests as a man may rest who has arisen from his ordinary life to effect some great deed of emancipation and deliverance, but, having accomplished it, returns again to the ordinary routine of his former life, glad and satisfied in his heart.

Nor is this rest for Christ alone, but for us also, who are forever identified with Him in His glorious life. We have been raised up together with Him in the mind and purpose of God, and have been made to sit with Him in the heavenlies, so that in Jesus we have already entered into the rest of God, and have simply to appropriate it by a living faith.

How, then, may we practically realise and enjoy the rest of God ?

(1) We must will the will of God. So long as the will of God, whether in the Bible or in providence, is going in one direction and our will in another, rest is impossible. Can there be rest in an earthly household when the children are ever chafing against the regulations and control of their parents? How much less can we be at rest if we harbour an incessant spirit of insubordination and questioning, contradicting and resisting the will of God!

That will must be done on earth as it is in heaven. None can stay His hand, or say, What are You doing? It will be done with us, or in spite of us. If we resist it, the yoke against which we rebel will only rub a sore place on our skin, but we must still carry it. How much wiser, then, meekly to yield to it, and submit ourselves under the mighty hand of God, saying, "Not my will, but Yours be done!"

The man who has learned the secret of Christ, in saying a perpetual "Yes" to the will of God; whose life is a strain of rich music to the theme, "Even so, Father", whose will follows the current of the will of God, as the smoke from our chimneys permits itself to be wafted by the winds of autumn, that man will find rest to his soul.

We must accept the finished work of Christ. He has ceased from the work of our redemption, because there was no more to do. Our sins and the sins of the world were put away. The power of the adversary was annulled. The gate of heaven was opened to all that believe. All was finished, and was very good.

Let us, then, cease from our works. Let us no longer feel as if we have to do aught, by our tears or prayers or works, to make ourselves acceptable to God. Why should we try to add one stitch to a finished garment, or append one stroke to the signed and sealed warrant of pardon placed within our hands?

We need have no anxiety as to the completeness or sufficiency of a divinely finished thing. Let us quiet our fears by considering that what satisfies Christ, our Saviour and Head, may well satisfy us. Let us dare to stand without a qualm in God's presence, by virtue of the glorious and completed sacrifice of Calvary. Let us silence every tremor of unrest by recalling the dying cry on the cross, and the witness of the empty grave.

We must trust our Father's care. "Casting all your care upon him, for He cares for you." Sometimes like a wild deluge, sweeping all before it, and sometimes like the continual dropping of water, so does care mar our peace. That we shall some day fall by the hand of Saul, that we shall be left to starve or pine away our days in a respectable workhouse, that we shall never be able to get through the difficulties of the coming days or weeks, household cares, family cares, business cares, cares about servants, children, money; crushing cares, and cares that buzz around the soul like a swarm of gnats on a summer's day, what rest can there be for a soul thus beset?

But, when we once learn to live by faith, believing that our Father loves us, and will not forget or forsake us, but is pledged to supply all our needs, when we acquire the holy habit of talking to Him about all, and handing over all to Him, at the moment that the tiniest shadow is cast upon the soul; when we accept insult and annoyance and interruption, coming to us from whatever quarter, as being by His permission, and, therefore, as part of His dear will for us, then we have learned the secret of the Gospel of Rest.

We must follow our Shepherd's lead. "We which have believed do enter into rest" (verse 3). The way is dark, the mountain track is often hidden from our sight by the heavy mists that hang over hill and fell, we can hardly discern a step in front. But our divine Guide knows.

He who trod earth's pathways is going unseen at our side. The shield of His environing protection is all around; and His voice, in its clear, sweet accents, is whispering peace. Why should we fear? He who touches us, touches His bride, His purchased possession, the apple of His eye. We may, therefore, trust and not be afraid.

Though the mountains should depart, or the hills be removed, yet will His loving kindness not depart from us, neither will the covenant of His peace be removed. And amid the storm, and darkness, and the onsets of our foes, we shall hear Him soothing us with the sweet refrain of His own lullaby of rest: "My peace I give to you. In the world you shall have tribulation, but in me you shall have peace."

CHAPTER 11: THE WORD OF GOD AND ITS EDGE

"The Word of God is quick and powerful, and sharper than any two-edged sword, piercing even to the dividing asunder of soul and spirit, and of the joints and marrow, and is a discerner of the thoughts and intents of the heart." (HEBREWS 4.12).

WE all have to do with God. "Him with whom we have to do." You cannot break the connection.

You must do with Him as a rebel, if not as a friend, on the ground of works, if not on the ground of grace, at the great white throne, if not in the fleeting days of time. You cannot do without God. You cannot do as you would if there were no God. You cannot avoid having to do with Him, for even though you were to say there was no God, doing violence to the clearest instincts of your being, yet still you would breathe His air, eat His provender, occupy His world, and stand at last before His bar.

And, if you will pardon the materialism of the reference, I will follow the suggestion of my text, and say that the God with Whom we have to do has eyes. "The eyes of Him with whom we have to do."

"You are a God Who sees" was the startled exclamation of an Egyptian slave girl whose childhood had been spent amid the vast statues of gods who had eyes with faraway stony stare, but saw not. And she was right. "The Lord looks from heaven; His eyes behold, His eyelids try, the children of men."

Those eyes miss no one. " There is not any creature not manifest in His sight." The truest goodness is least obtrusive of itself. It steals unnoticed through the world, filling up its days with deeds and words of gentle kindness, which are known only to heaven. And herein it finds its sufficient reward. It prays behind closed doors, it exercises a vigorous self-denial in secret, it does its work of mercy by stealth.

Thus the great blatant world of men, with its trumpets and heralds and newspaper notices, knows little of it, and cannot find the nooks where God's wild flowers bloom in inaccessible heights for His eye alone.

But the Father sees in secret. The eyes of the Lord are upon the righteous. His eyes run to and fro throughout the whole earth, to show Himself strong on behalf of those whose heart is perfect toward Him. Do you want guidance? Look up! those eyes wait to guide by a glance. Are you in sorrow? They will film with tears. Are you going astray? They shall beckon you back, and break your heart, as they did Peter's. You will come to find your heaven in the light radiated by the eye of God, when once you have learned to meet it, clad in the righteousness of Jesus.

Unconverted reader, remember there is no screen from the eye of God. His eyes are as a flame of fire; and our strongest screens crackle up as thinnest gauze before the touch of that holy flame. Even rocks and hills are inadequate to hide from the face of Him that sits upon the throne.

"Where shall I go from Your presence?" That question is unanswered, and unanswerable. It has stood upon the page of Scripture for three thousand years, and no one yet of all the myriads that have read it has been able to devise a reply.

Heaven says, 'Not here'. Hell says, 'Not here'. It is not among angels, or the lost, or in the vast silent spaces of eternity. There is no creature anywhere not manifest to His sight. He who made vultures, able from immense heights to discern the least morsel on the desert waste, has eyes as good as they.

And think how terrible are the eyes of God! When Egypt's chivalry had pursued Israel into the depths of the sea, they suddenly turned to flee. Why? Not because of thunder or lightning or voice; but because of a look. "The Lord looked out of the cloud, and troubled the Egyptians."

Ah, sinner, how terrible will it be for you to abide under the frown of God! "With the perverse and refractory He will show himself perverse and refractory."

Those eyes miss nothing. "All things are naked and opened to the eyes of Him with whom we have to do." It is said of the Lord Jesus, on one occasion, that He entered into Jerusalem, and into the Temple, and 'when He had looked round about on all things', He went out. It was His last, long, farewell look. But note its comprehensiveness. Nothing escaped it.

We look only on parts of things, and often look without seeing. But the Lord sees not as man sees, for man looks on the outward appearance, but the Lord looks on the heart.

"Naked and opened." This is a sacrificial phrase, indicating the priestly act of throwing the victim on its back before him, so that it lay, exposed to his gaze, helpless to recover itself, ready for the knife.

Ah, how eagerly we try to hide and cloak our sin! We dare not pen a truthful diary. We dread the illness which would unlock our tongues in wholesale chatterings. We shrink from the loving gaze of our dearest. We deceive man, and sometimes ourselves - but not our great High-Priest. He sees all. That secret sin, that lurking enmity, that closed chamber, that hidden burglar, that masked assassin, that stowaway, that declension of heart, that little rift within the lute, that speck of decay in the luscious fruit.

And thus it is that men are kept out of the Canaan of God's rest, because He sees the evil heart of unbelief which departs from Himself, and on account of which He swears now, as of old, "they shall not enter into My rest."

Is it not a marvel that He who knows so much about us should love us still. It were indeed an inexplicable mystery, save for the truth of the words which so sweetly follow: "Seeing, then, that we have a great High-Priest." He has a priest's heart. His scrutiny is not one of morbid or idle curiosity, but of a surgeon, who intently examines the source of disease with pity and tenderness, and resolves to extirpate it as quickly and as painlessly as possible.

Is it not frequently the case that fuller knowledge will beget love, which once seemed impossible? There are some people whose faces are so hard, and their eyes so cold, that we are instantly repelled, but if we knew all, how they have been pierced and wounded, and disappointed, we should begin to pity them, and pity is close kinsman to love.

The Saviour has known us from all eternity, our downsittings and uprisings, our secret possibilities of evil, our unfathomed depths of waywardness and depravity, and yet He loves us, and will love us.

"He knows all, But loves us better than He knows."

And out of this love, which wells up perennially in the heart of Jesus, unfrozen by the winter of our neglect, unstaunched by the demands of our fickleness, there comes the stern discipline of which this passage proceeds to speak.

In majestic phrase, the Apocalyptic seer tells how he beheld the Word of God ride forth on his snow-white steed, arrayed in crimson robes, whilst the many crowns of empire flashed upon His brow.

Two features are specially noted in his appearance. 'His eyes were as a flame of fire'. This characteristic looks back over the words we have considered. 'Out of his mouth goes a sharp two-edged sword'. This looks forward to the words which now invite us.

We must never divorce these two. The eyes and the sword. Not the eyes only, for of what use would it be to see and not strike? Not the sword only, for to strike without seeing would give needless pain. This would be surgery blindfolded. But the searching tender vision, followed by the swift and decisive flash of the sword of amputation and deliverance.

Oh, who will now submit to that stroke, wielded by the gentle hand that often carried healing and blessing, and was nailed to the cross, guided by unerring wisdom, and nerved by Almighty strength? Not death, but life and fruitfulness, freedom and benediction, are all awaiting that one blow of emancipation. That sword is the Word of God.

THE WORD OF GOD IS LIVING. The words He speaks are spirit and life (John 6.63). Wherever they fall, though into dull and lifeless soil, they begin to breed life, and produce results like themselves.

They come into the heart of an abandoned woman; and straightway there follow compunction for the past, vows of amendment, and the hasty rush to become an evangelist to others. They come into the heart of a dying robber; and immediately he refrains from blasphemy, and rebukes his fellow, and announces the Messiahship, the blamelessness, the approaching glory, of the dying Saviour. They come into hearts worn out with the wild excesses of the great pagan ages, and ill-content, though enriched with the spoils of art and refinement and philosophy in the very zenith of their development, and lo! the moral waste begins to sprout with harvests of holiness, and to blossom with the roses of heaven.

If only those words, spoken from the lips of Christ, be allowed to work in the conscience, there will be forthwith the stir of life.

THE WORD OF GOD IS ACTIVE, i.e., energetic. Beneath its spell the blind see, the deaf hear, the paralysed are nerved with new energy, the dead stir in their graves and come forth.

There are few things more energetic than life. Put a seed into the fissure of a rock, and it will split it in two from top to bottom. Though walls and rocks and ruins impede the course of the seedling, yet it will force its way to the light and air and rain. And when the Word of God enters the heart, it is not as a piece of furniture or lumber. It asserts itself and strives for mastery, and compels men to give up sin, to make up long-standing feuds, to restore ill-gotten gains, to strive to enter into the strait gate.

"Now you are pruned," said our Lord, "through the word that I have spoken to you." The words of Christ are His winnowing-fan, with which He is wont to purge his flour, whether in the heart or the world. We are not, therefore, surprised that a leading tradesman in a thriving commercial centre said that the visit of two evangelists, who did little else than reiterate the Word of God, was as good as a revival of trade, because it led so many people to pay up debts which were reckoned as lost.

THE WORD OF GOD IS SHARP. Its sharpness is threefold. It is sharp to pierce. On the day of Pentecost, as Peter wielded the sword of the Spirit, it pierced three thousand to the heart; and they fell wounded to the death before him, crying, "What shall we do?"

Often since have strong men been smitten to the dust under the effect of that same sword, skilfully used. And this is the kind of preaching we need. Men are urged to accept of the gift of God, and many seem to comply with the invitation, but in the process of time they fall away. Is not the cause in this, that they have never been wounded to the death of their self-esteem, their heart has never been pierced to the letting of the blood of their own life, they have never been brought into the dust of death?

Oh for Boanerges! able to pierce the armour of excuses, of vain hopes behind which men shield themselves, that many may cry with Ahab, pierced between the joints of the harness "Turn your hand, and carry me out of the battle, for I am wounded!"

It is sharp to divide. With his sharp knife the priest was accustomed to dissect the joints of the animal, and to open to view even the marrow of the bones. Every hair was searched, every limb examined, and thus the sacred gift was passed, and permitted to be offered in worship.

And God's scrutiny is not satisfied with the external appearance and profession. It goes far deeper. It enters into those mysterious regions of the nature where soul and spirit, purpose, intention, motive, and impulse, hold their secret court, and carry on the hidden machinery of human life.

Who can tread the mysterious confines where soul and spirit touch? What is the line of demarcation? Where does the one end, and the other begin? We cannot tell. But that mystic Word of God could cut the one from the other, as easily as the selvage is divided from the cloth. It is at home in distinctions which are too fine drawn and minute for human apprehension. It assumes an office like that which Jesus refused when He said, "Who made me a judge and divider over you?"

It is sharp to criticise and judge. "Quick to discern the thoughts and intents of the heart." Christ is eager about these. Because what a man thinks and intends in his heart, that he will be sooner or later in life. We must expect to have our most secret thoughts, relations, and purposes questioned, criticised, and measured by the Word of God.

No court of inquiry was ever presided over by a more exact inquisitor than this. The corpses of the dead past are exhumed, the old lumber-rooms with their padlocked boxes are explored, the accounts of bygone years are audited and taxed.

God is critic of all the secrets of the heart. As each thought or intention passes to and fro, He searches it. He is constantly weighing in the balance our thoughts and aims, though they be light as air.

On one occasion, when Saul had spared the spoils of a doomed city, together with its monarch, the latter came to Samuel, not as a criminal, but delicately, as a pampered friend. And Samuel said, "As your sword has made women childless, so shall your mother be childless among women. And Samuel hewed Agag in pieces before the Lord." Thus it is that we have spared too many of our sins, at the risk of our irreparable rejection from the throne of true manhood and righteousness.

How much better to let Christ do His work of amputation and excision! If we do not know ourselves, let us ask Him to search us. If we cannot cut off the offending member, let us look to Him to rid us of it.

Do not fear Him. Close after these terrible words, as the peal of bells after the crash of the storm on the organ at Freiburg, we are told that "He was tempted in all points like as we are," and that "we have not a High Priest who cannot be touched with the feeling of our infirmities."

"Does she sing well?" asked the trainer of a new operatic singer. "Splendidly," was the reply; "but if I had to bring her out, I would first break her heart." He meant that one who had not been broken by sorrow could not touch the deepest chords of human life.

Ah! there is no need for this with our Lord Jesus. Reproach broke his heart. He understands broken hearts, and is able to soothe and save all who come unto God by Him.

CHAPTER 12: TIMELY AND NEEDED HELP

"Let us therefore come boldly to the throne of grace, that we may obtain mercy, and find grace to help in time of need." (HEBREWS 4.16).

NEED! Time of need! Every hour we live is a time of need, and we are safest and happiest when we feel our needs most keenly.

If you say that you are rich, and increased in goods, and have need of nothing, you are in the greatest destitution. But when you know yourself to be wretched, miserable, poor, blind, and naked, then the travelling merchant is already standing on your doorstep, knocking (Revelation 3.17-20). It is when the supply runs short, that Cana's King makes the vessels brim with wine.

Have you been convinced of your need? If not, it is quite likely that you will live and die without a glimpse of the rich provision which God has made to meet it.

Of what use is it to talk of rich provisions and sumptuous viands to those already satiated? But when the soul, by the straits of its necessity, has been brought to the verge of desperation, when we cry with the lepers of old, "If we say we will enter into the city, then the famine is in the city, and we shall die there; and if we sit still here, we die also", then we are on the verge of discovering the rich provision that awaits us (2 Kings 7.8) - 'all spiritual blessings' in the heavenlies (Ephesians 1.3); and 'all things that pertain to life and godliness' (2 Peter 1.3).

There are two causes, therefore, why many Christians are living such impoverished lives. They have never realised their own infinite need, and they have never availed themselves of those infinite resources which hang within their reach, like fruit from the stooping boughs of an orchard in autumn.

Our needs are twofold. We need mercy. This is our fundamental need. Mercy when we are at our worst, yes, and at our best, mercy when the pruning knife cuts deep, yes, and when we are covered with foliage, flower, or fruit, mercy when we are broken and sore vexed, yes, and when we stand on the paved sapphire work upon the mountain summit to talk with God. The greatest saint among us can no more exist without the mercy of God than the ephemeral insects of a summer's noon can live without the sun.

We need grace to help. Help to walk through the valleys, and to walk on the high places, where the chamois can hardly stand. Help to suffer, to be still, to wait, to overcome, to make green one tiny spot of garden ground in God's great tillage. Help to live and to die.

Each of these is met at the throne. Come, let us go to it. It is not the great white throne of judgment, but the rainbow-girt throne of grace.

"No," you cry, "never! I am a man of unclean lips and heart. I dare not face Him before Whom angels veil their faces. The fire of His awful purity will leap out on me, shrivelling and consuming. I exceedingly fear and quake. Or, if I muster courage enough to go once, I shall never be able to go as often as I need, or to ask for the common and trivial gifts required in daily living."

Hush, soul! you may approach as often and as boldly as you will, for we have a great High Priest, Who is passed through the heavens, and not one who cannot be touched with the feeling of our infirmities.

A PRIEST. - Deep down in the heart of men there is a strong and instinctive demand for a priest, to be daysman and mediator, to lay one hand on man and the other on God, and to go between them both. Wit and sarcasm may launch their epithets on this primordial craving, but they might as well try to extinguish by the same methods the craving of the body for food, of the understanding for truth, of the heart for love.

And no religion is destined to meet the deepest yearnings of the race, which does not have glowing at the heart the provision of a priest to stand before the throne of grace, as, of old, the priest stood before the mercy seat, which was its literal prefiguration under the dispensation of the Levitical law.

A curious proof of this human craving for a priest is given in the book of Judges. On the ridge of the hills of Ephraim stood the ancestral home of a wealthy family, containing within its precincts a private sanctuary, where though there were teraphim, ephod, and vestments, yet there was no priest. Nothing, however, could compensate for that fatal lack.

And Micah said to a Levite, who happened to pass by: "Dwell with me, and be unto me a father and a priest." And when he, nothing loath, consented, Micah comforted himself by saying, "Now know I that the Lord will do me good, seeing I have a Levite to my priest."

But the same feelings that actuated him were shared by a portion of the tribe of Dan, on their way to colonise a remote part of the country. They, too, must have a priest; and so, while six hundred armed warriors stood around the gate, five men stole through the court, broke into the little chapel, carried off its images and other apparatus for worship, bribed the priest, by the offer of a higher wage, to accompany them, and, long before the theft was discovered, the whole party had resumed their journey, and were far upon their way.

All families of mankind have followed the same general programme . Wherever they have built homes for themselves, they have erected the wigwam, the pagoda, the parthenon, the obelisk guarded temple, the Gothic minster fashioned after the model of the forest glade, a leafy oracle petrified to stone. And they have chosen one of themselves, set apart from ordinary work, and sanctified by special rites to minister, treading its floors, and pleading at its altars, interceding for them in times of famine, pestilence, and plague, blessing their arms as they went forth to fight, and receiving their spoils of victory; making propitiation for sin, and assuring of forgiveness.

This craving was most carefully met in that venerable religion in which these Hebrew Christians had been reared. The sons of Aaron were the priests of Israel. They wore a special dress, ate special food, and lived in special towns, whilst every care was taken to accentuate their separation to transact the spiritual concerns of the nation.

For sixteen centuries this system had prevailed, rallying around it the deepest and most sacred emotions, and, like ivy, entwining itself around the oak of the national life. And, as we have seen, it was no small privation for these new converts to wrench themselves from such a system, and accept a religion in which there was no visible temple, ceremonial, or priest.

But here we learn that Jesus Christ is the perfect answer to these instinctive cravings which blindly pointed to Him in all ages of human and Hebrew history.

This is the aim of these opening chapters, and by two lines of proof we have been led to the same conclusion. Before us stand two mighty columns: the one is in chapters 1 and 2 of this Epistle, the other is in 3 and 4. They have a common base from which they spring, the Sonship of Christ.

The first column is called, Christ superior to Angels; and this is the scroll around its capital, that Jesus, as man's representative, has entered into the glories promised in the eighth Psalm.

The second column is called, Christ superior to Moses; with this scroll around its capital, that Jesus, as our representative, has entered into the Rest of God. And each of them helps to support a common chapter, the Priesthood of Christ.

The first two chapters end with a description of the merciful and faithful High Priest, who makes reconciliation for the sins of the people (2.17, 18). The next two chapters close with the words on which we are dwelling now, concerning the Great High-Priest (4.14).

In the mouth of two witnesses every word is established. We need no human priests. Their work is done, their office is superseded, their functions are at an end. To arrogate any priestly functions of sacrifice, of absolution, or of imparting sacramental grace, is to intrude sacrilegiously on ground which is sacred to the Son of God; and, however royal such are in mien or intellect, they must be withstood, as Azariah withstood Uzziah, saying, "It does not appertain to you to burn incense to the Lord, but to Jesus, our Great High-Priest. Go out of His office, for you have trespassed, neither shall it be for your honour from the Lord God."

A HIGH PRIEST. A Priest of priests, able to sacrifice, not only for the people, but for all the priests of his house, and alone responsible for the rites of the great day of Atonement, when every other priest was banished from the precincts of the Temple, while the high priest, clad in simple white, made an atonement for the sins of himself, his family, and his people.

We have been made priests to God, but our priestly work consists in the offering of the incense of prayer and praise, and the gifts of surrendered lives. We have nothing to do with atonement for sin, which is urgently required by us, not only for our sins as ordinary members of the congregation, but for those which, consciously or unconsciously, we commit in the exercise of our priestly office.

Our penitential tears need to be sprinkled by the blood of Jesus, our holiest hours need to be accepted through His merits, our noblest service would condemn us, save for His atoning sacrifice.

A GREAT HIGH PRIEST. All other high priests were inferior to Him. He is as much superior to the high priests as any one of them was to the priests of his time. But this does not exhaust His greatness. He does not belong to their line at all, but to an older, more venerable, and grander one, of which that mysterious personage was the founder, to whom Abraham, the father of Israel, gave tithes and homage.

"Declared of God a High Priest after the order of Melchizedek." Nay, further, His greatness is that of the Son of God, the fellow and equal of Deity. He is as great as His infinite nature and the divine appointment and His ideal of ministry could make Him.

PASSED THROUGH THE HEAVENS. Between the holy place where the priest daily performed the service of the sanctuary, and the inner shrine forbidden to all save to the high priest once each year, there hung a veil of blue. And of what was that blue veil the emblem, save of those heavenly curtains, the work of God's fingers, which hang between our mortal vision and the marvels of His presence chamber?

Once a year the high priest carried the blood of propitiation through the blue veil of separation, and sprinkled it upon the mercy seat; and in this significant and solemn act he typified the entrance of our blessed Lord into the immediate presence of God, bearing the marks and emblems of His atoning death, and taking up His position there as our Mediator and Intercessor, in Whom we are represented, and for Whose sake we are accepted and beloved.

TOUCHED WITH THE FEELING OF OUR INFIRMITIES. He hates the sin, but loves the sinner. His hatred to the one is measured by His cross; His love to the other is as infinite as His nature. And His love is not a dreamy ecstasy, but practical, because all the machinery of temptation was brought into operation against Him.

It would take too long to enumerate the points at which the great adversary of souls assails us; but there is not a sense, a faculty, a power, which may not be the avenue of his attack. Through eye-gate, ear-gate, and thought-gate his squadrons seek to pour. And, marvellous though it be, yet our High Priest was tempted in all these points, in body, soul, and spirit; though there was no faltering in His holy resolution, no vacillation or shadow of turning, no desire to yield. "The prince of this world comes, and has nothing in me."

All His experiences are vividly present to Him still, and whenever we go to Him, pleading for mercy or help, He instantly knows just how much and where we need it, and immediately His intercessions obtain for us, and His hands bestow, the exact form of either we may require.

"He is touched." That sympathetic heart is the metropolis to which each afferent nerve carries an immediate thrill from the meanest and remotest members of His body, bringing at once in return the very help and grace which are required.

Oh to live in touch with Christ! always touching Him, as of old the women touched His garment's hem, and receiving responses, quick as the lightning flash, and full of the healing, saving virtue of God (Mark 5.28).

CHAPTER 13: GETHSEMANE

"Who in the days of his flesh, when he had offered up prayers and supplications with strong crying and tears unto him that was able to save him from death, and was heard in that he feared: though he were a Son, yet learned he obedience by the things which he suffered." (HEBREWS 5.7-8).

Eight ancient olive trees still mark the site of Gethsemane. Not improbably they witnessed that memorable and mysterious scene referred to here. And what a scene was that! It had stood alone in unique and unapproachable wonder, had it not been followed by fifteen hours of even greater mystery.

The strongest words in Greek language are used to tell of the keen anguish through which the Saviour passed within those Garden walls.

"He began to be sorrowful", as if in all His past experiences He had never known what sorrow was!

"He was sore amazed", as if His mind were almost dazed and overwhelmed.

"He was very heavy," His spirit stooped beneath the weight of his sorrows, as afterward His body stooped beneath the weight of His cross, or the word may mean that He was so distracted with sorrow, as to be almost beside Himself. And the Lord Himself could not have found a stronger word than He used when He said, "My soul is exceeding sorrowful, even to death."

But the evangelist Luke gives us the most convincing proof of His anguish when he tells us that His sweat, like great beads of blood, fell upon the ground, touched by the slight frost, and in the cold night air. The finishing touch is given in these words, which tell of His "strong crying and tears."

THE THINGS WHICH HE SUFFERED. What were they? They were not those of the Substitute. The tenor of Scripture goes to show that the work of substitution was really wrought out upon the cross. There the robe of our completed righteousness was woven from the top throughout.

It was on the tree that He bare our sins in His own body. It was by His blood that He brought us nigh to God. It was by the death of God's Son that we have been reconciled to God. And the repeated references of Scripture, and especially of this epistle, to sacrifice, indicate that in the act of dying, that was done which magnifies the law, and makes it honourable, and removes every obstacle that had otherwise prevented the love of God from following out its purposes of mercy.

We shall never fully understand here how the Lord Jesus made reconciliation for the sins of the world, or how that which He bore could be an equivalent for the penalty due from a sinful race.

We have no standard of comparison. We have no line long enough to let us down into the depths of that unexplored mystery; but we may thankfully accept it as a fact stated on the page of Scripture perpetually, that He did that which put away the curse, atoned for human guilt, and was more than equivalent to all those sufferings which a race of sinful men must otherwise have borne.

The mystery defies our language, but it is apprehended by faith, and as she stands upon her highest pinnacles, love discerns the meaning of the death of Christ by a spiritual instinct, though as yet she has not perfectly learned the language in which to express her conceptions of the mysteries that circle around the cross. It may be that in thousands of unselfish actions, she is acquiring the terms in which some day she will be able to understand and explain all.

But all that we need insist on here and now, is that the sufferings of the Garden are not to be included in the act of Substitution, though, as we shall see, they were closely associated with it. Gethsemane was not the altar, but the way to it.

Our Lord's suffering in Gethsemane could hardly arise from the fear of His approaching physical sufferings. Such a supposition seems wholly inconsistent with the heroic fortitude, the majestic silence, the calm ascendancy over suffering with which He bore Himself till He breathed out His spirit, and which drew from a hardened and worldly Roman expressions of respect.

Besides, if the mere prospect of scourging and crucifixion drew from our Lord these strong crying and tears and bloody sweat, He surely would stand on a lower level than that to which multitudes of His followers attained through faith in Him.

Old men like Polycarp, tender maidens like Blandina, timid boys like Attalus, have contemplated beforehand with unruffled composure, and have endured with unshrinking fortitude, deaths far more awful, more prolonged, more agonising. Degraded criminals have climbed the scaffold without a tremor or a sob, and surely the most exalted faith ought to bear itself as bravely as the most brutal indifference in the presence of the solemnities of death and eternity.

It has been truly said that there is no passion in the mind of man, however weak, which cannot master the fear of death; and it is therefore impossible to suppose that the fear of physical suffering and disgrace could have so shaken our Saviour's spirit.

But He anticipated the sufferings that He was to endure as the propitiation for sin. He knew that He was about to be brought into the closest association with the sin which was devastating human happiness and grieving the divine nature.

He knew, since He had so identified Himself with our fallen race, that, in a very deep and wonderful way, He was to be made sin and to bear our curse and shame, cast out by man, and apparently forsaken by God.

He knew, as we shall never know, the exceeding sinfulness and horror of sin, and what it was to be the meeting-place where the iniquities of our race should converge, to become the scapegoat charged with guilt not his own, to bear away the sins of the world. All this was beyond measure terrible to one so holy and sensitive as He.

He had long foreseen it. He was the Lamb slain from before the foundation of the world. Each time a lamb was slain by a conscience-stricken sinner, or a scapegoat let go into the wilderness, or a pigeon dipped into the flowing water encrimsoned by the blood of its mate, He had been reminded of what was to be.

He knew before His incarnation where in the forest the seedling was growing to a sapling from the wood of which His cross would be made. He even nourished it with His rain and sun.

Often during His public ministry He was evidently looking beyond the events that were transpiring around Him to that supreme event, which He called His "hour." And as it came nearer, His human soul was overwhelmed at the prospect of having to sustain the weight of a world's sin.

His human nature did not shrink from death as death, but from the death which He was to die as the propitiation for our sins, and not for ours only, but for those of the whole world.

Six months before His death He had set His face to go to Jerusalem, with such a look of anguish upon it as to fill the hearts of His disciples with consternation.

When the questions of the Greeks reminded Him that He must shortly fall into the ground and die, His soul became so troubled that He cried, "Father, save me from this hour !"

And now, with strong cryings and tears, He made supplication to His Father, as king, that, if it were possible, the cup might pass from Him.

In this His human soul spoke. As to His divinely wrought purpose of redemption, there was no vacillation or hesitation. But, as man, He asked whether there might not be another way of accomplishing the redemption on which He had set his heart.

But there was no other way. The Father's will, which He had come down from heaven to do, pointed along the rugged, flinty road that climbed Calvary, and passed over it, and down to the grave. And at once He accepted His destiny, and with the words "If this cup may not pass from me except I drink it, Your will be done," He stepped forth on the flints that were to cut those blessed feet, drawing from them streams of blood.

HIS STRONG CRYING AND TEARS. Our Lord betook Himself to that resource which is within the reach of all, and which is peculiarly precious to those who are suffering and tempted, He prayed. His heart was overwhelmed within Him, and He poured out all His anguish into His Father's ears, with strong cryings and tears. Let us note the characteristics of that prayer, that we too may be able to pass through our dark hours, when they come.

It was secret prayer. Leaving the majority of His disciples at the Garden gate, He took with Him the three who had stood beside Jairus's dead child, and had beheld the radiance that steeped Him in His transfiguration. They alone might see Him tread the winepress; but even they were left at a stone's cast, whilst He went forward alone into the deeper shadow.

We are told that they became overpowered with sleep, so that no mortal ear heard the whole burden of that marvellous prayer, some fitful snatches of which are reserved in the Gospels.

It was humble prayer. The evangelist Luke says that He knelt. Another says that He fell on his face. Being formed in fashion as a man, He humbled Himself and became obedient to death, even the death of the cross. And it may be that even then He began to recite that marvellous Psalm, which was so much on His lips during those last hours, saying, "I am a worm, and no man, a reproach of men and despised of the people."

It was filial prayer. Matthew describes our Lord as saying, "Oh my Father", and Mark tells us that He used the endearing term which was often spoken by the prattling lips of little Jewish children, Abba. For the most part, He probably spoke Greek. But Aramaic was the language of His childhood, the language of the dear home in Nazareth.

In the hour of mortal agony, the mind ever reverts to the associations of its first awakening. The Saviour, therefore, appearing to feel that the more stately Greek did not sufficiently express the deep yearnings of His heart, substituted for it the more tender language of earlier years. Not "Father" only, but "Abba, Father!"

It was earnest prayer. "He prayed more earnestly," and one proof of this appears in His repetition of the same words. It was as if His nature were too oppressed to be able to express itself in a variety of phrase, such as might indicate a certain leisure and liberty of thought. One strong current of anguish running at its highest could only strike one monotone of grief, like the note of the storm or the flood. Back, and back again, came the words, cup . .pass . . . will . . . Father. And the sweat of blood, pressed from His forehead, as the red juice of the grape beneath the heavy foot of the peasant, witnessed to the intensity of His soul.

It was submissive prayer. Matthew and Mark quote this sentence, "Nevertheless not what I will, but what You will." Luke quotes this, "Father, if You be willing, remove this cup from me, nevertheless, not my will, but Your's be done."

Jesus was the Father's Fellow, co-equal in His divine nature, but for the purpose of redemption it was needful that He should temporarily divest Himself of the use of the attributes of His deity, and live a truly human life.

As man, He carefully marked each symptom of His Father's will, from the day when it prompted Him to linger behind His parents in the temple, and He always instantly fulfilled His behests. "I came down from heaven," He said, "not to do mine own will, but the will of him that sent me." This was the yoke He bore, and in taking it, He found rest unto His soul.

Whatever was the danger or difficulty into which such obedience might carry Him, He ever followed the beacon-cloud of the divine will, sure that the manna of daily strength would fall, and that the deep sweet waters of peace would follow where it led the way.

That way now seemed to lead through the heart of a fiery furnace. There was no alternative than to follow, and He elected to do so, nay, was glad, even then, with a joy that the cold waters of death could not extinguish.

At the same time, He learnt what obedience meant, and gave an example of it, that shone out with unequalled majesty, purity, and beauty, unparalleled in the annals of the universe. As man, our Lord then learnt how much was meant by that word obedience.

"He learned obedience." And now He asks that we should obey Him, as He obeyed God. "To them that obey him."

Sometimes the path of the Christian's obedience becomes very difficult. It climbs upward. The gradient is continually steeper. The foothold ever more difficult. And, as the evening comes, the nimble climber of the morning creeps slowly forward on hands and knees. The day is never greater than the strength, but as the strength grows by use, the demands upon it are greater, and the hours longer.

At last a moment may come, when we are called for God's sake to leave some dear circle, to risk the loss of name and fame, to relinquish the cherished ambition of a life, to incur obloquy, suffering, and death, to drink the bitter cup, to enter the brooding cloud, to climb the smoking mount. Ah! then we too learn what obedience means; and have no resource but in strong cryings and tears.

In such hours pour out your heart in audible cries. Plentifully mingle the name "Father" with your entreaties. Fear not to repeat the same words. Look not to man, he cannot understand you, but to Him who is nearer to you than your dearest. So shall you get calmer and quieter, until you rest in His will, as a child, worn out by a tempest of passion, sobs itself to sleep on its mother's breast.

THE ANSWER. "He was heard for His godly fear." His holy reverence and devotion to His Father's will made it impossible that His prayers should be unanswered, although, as it so often happens, the answer came in another way than His fears had suggested. The cup was not taken away, but the answer came. It came in the mission of the angel that stood beside Him. It came in the calm serenity with which He met the brutal crowd, that soon filled that quiet Garden with their coarse voices and trampling feet. It came in His triumph over death and the grave. It came in His being perfected as mediator, to become unto all them that obey Him the Author of eternal salvation, and the High-Priest forever after the order of Melchizedek.

Prayers prompted by love and in harmony with godly fear are never lost. We may ask for things which it would be unwise and unkind of God to grant; but in that case, His goodness shows itself rather in the refusal than the assent.

And yet the prayer is heard and answered. Strength is instilled into the fainting heart. The faithful and merciful High-Priest does for us what the angel essayed to do for Him; but how much better, since He has learnt so much of the art of comfort in the school of suffering!

And out of it the way finally emerges into life, though we have left the right hand and foot in the grave behind us. We also discover that we have learnt the art of becoming channels of eternal salvation to those around us.

Ever since Jesus suffered there, Gethsemane has been threaded by the King's highway that passes through it to the New Jerusalem. And in its precincts God has kept many of His children, to learn obedience by the things that they suffer, and to learn the divine art of comforting others as they themselves have been comforted by God.

There are comparatively few, to whom Jesus does not say, at some time in their lives, "Come and watch with me." He takes us with Him into the darksome shadows of the winepress, though there are recesses of shade, at a stone's cast, where He must go alone. Let us not misuse the precious hours in the heavy slumbers of insensibility. There are lessons to be learnt there which can be acquired nowhere else. But if we heed not His summons to watch with Him, it may be that He will close the precious opportunity by bidding us sleep on and take our rest, because the allotted term has passed, and the hour of a new epoch has struck.

If we fail to use for prayer and preparation the sacred hour, that comes laden with opportunities for either; if we sleep instead of watching with our Lord, what hope have we of being able to play a noble part when the flashing lights and the trampling feet announce the traitor's advent? Squander the moments of preparation, and you may have to rue their loss through all the coming years!

CHAPTER 14: IMPOSSIBLE TO RENEW TO REPENTANCE

"It is impossible for those who were once enlightened, and have tasted of the heavenly gift, and were made partakers of the Holy Ghost, and have tasted the good word of God, and the powers of the world to come, if they shall fall away, to renew them again unto repentance; seeing they crucify to themselves the Son of God afresh, and put him to an open shame." (HEBREWS 6.4-6.)

The sacred writer enumerates four fundamental principles: Repentance from dead works, which in the old dispensation was symbolised by divers baptisms, or washings. Faith toward God, typified by the laying of hands on the head of the victim-sacrifices. The Resurrection of the dead, and Eternal Judgment. And then he proposes not to lay them again, but to leave them. There is no thought, however, of deserting them. The great principles on which God saves the soul are identical in every age, and indispensable.

We can only leave them as the child leaves the multiplication-table, when it is well learnt, but which lies at the root of all after-study, as the plant leaves the root when it towers into the majestic shrub, which draws all its life from that low origin; and as the builder leaves the foundation, that he may carry up stone on stone, and leans on the foundation most heavily, when he has left it at the furthest distance below him.

And we are taught the reason why these principles are not laid afresh. It would be useless to do so. It would serve no good purpose. It would leave in the same state as it found them those who had apostatised from the faith.

And so we are led to one of those passages which sensitive spirits have turned to their own torment and anguish, just as men will distil the rankest poison from some of the sweetest flowers.

HOW FAR WE MAY GO, AND YET FALL AWAY. These apostate disciples had been enlightened (verse 4). They had been led to see their sin and danger, the temporary nature of Judaism, the dignity and glory of the Saviour. Other Hebrews might be ignorant, the folds of the veil hanging heavily over their sight, but it could never be so with them, since they had stood in the midst of the Gospel's meridian light, and had been enlightened.

So may it be with us. Not like the savage, crouching before his fetish, or roaming over the wild; not like the follower of Confucius, Buddha, or Mahomet, groping in the twilight of nature or religious guesswork, not like myriads in our own land, whose hearts are as dark as the chaos into which God commanded the primeval beam to shine. We have been enlightened.

We may know that we are sinners. We may have learnt from childhood the scheme of salvation. We may be familiar with the mysteries of the kingdom of heaven, into which angels desire to look. And yet we may fall away.

These Hebrews, here referred to, had also tasted of the heavenly gift. What gift is that? I hear a voice, which we know well, speaking from the well of Sychar, and saying: "The water that I will give shall be in you, springing up into everlasting life." It is the life of God in the soul. It is Christ Himself. And He is willing to be in us, like a perennial spring, unstaunched in drought, unfrozen in frost, leaping up, in fresh and living beauty, like some warm spring that makes a paradise in the arctic circle.

But some are content not to receive it, only to taste it. This is what these persons did. They sipped the sweetness of Christ. They had a passing superficial glimpse into His heart. Like Gideon's soldiers, they caught up a few drops in their hands from the river of God, and hastened on their way.

So we may have some pleasure in thoughts of Christ. His sufferings touch, His beauty attracts, His history moves and inspires. But it is only a taste; and yet we may fall away.

They had also been made partakers of the Holy Ghost. It is not said that they had been converted, regenerated, or filled by the Holy Ghost. The expression is a very peculiar one, and it is used because the sacred writer could not affirm any of these things of them, and yet was anxious to show that they had been brought under His gracious influences.

For instance, He had convinced them of sin, had striven with them, had plied them with warning and entreaty, with fear and hope. And they had so far yielded to Him as to give up some of their sins and assume the outward guise of Christianity.

Moreover, they had tasted the good Word of God, and the powers of the world to come. The first of these is obviously the Scriptures, and the second is the usual expression for the age in which we live, and which, with all its spiritual forces, was beginning to thrill the hearts of men when these words were penned. They liked a good sermon. The Bible was full of interest and charm. They had heard the prophets, and seen the apostles of the Pentecostal age. All these had been analysed, weighed, and counted. And yet they were in peril of going back. Let us, therefore, beware!

WHAT IS IT TO FALL AWAY? It is something more than to fall. The real child of God may fall, as David or as Peter did, but there is a vast difference between falling and falling away. This latter experience can no more come to a real believer than a second flood of waters to the earth, but it will certainly find out the counterfeit and the sham.

To fall away is to go back from the outward profession of Christianity, not temporarily, but finally; not as the result of some sudden sin, but because the first outward stimulus is exhausted, and there is no true life beating at the heart, to repair or reinvigorate the wasting devotion of the life.

It is to resemble those wandering planets, which never shone with their own light, but only in the reflected light of some central sun, but which, having broken from its guiding leash, dash further and further into the blackness of darkness, without one spark of life or heat or light. It is to return as a dog to its vomit, and as a sow to her filth, because the reformation was only outward and temporary, and the dog or sow natures were never changed through the gracious work of the Holy Spirit.

It is to be another Judas. To commit the sin against the Holy Spirit. To lose all earnestness of feeling, all desire for better things, all power of tender emotion, and to become utterly callous and dead, as the pavement on which we walk, or the rusty armour hanging on the old castle's walls.

WHY IT IS IMPOSSIBLE TO RESTORE SUCH TO REPENTANCE. Notice, there is nothing said here of what God can do. The only question is as to the limits of human power, and the ordinary methods of influencing human wills.

Also notice, we are not told that God could not save those who had fallen away, but that it is impossible to hope that a man who has passed through the experiences just described, and has nevertheless apostatised, can be reached or touched by any of those arguments or motives which are familiar weapons in the Gospel armoury.

If the mightiest arguments have been brought to bear on the conscience in vain, if after some slight response, which gave hopes of better things, it has relapsed into the stupor and insensibility of its former state, there remains nothing more to be done.

There is nothing more potent than the wail of Calvary's broken heart, and the peal from Sinai's brow; and, if these have been tried in vain, no argument is left which can touch the conscience and arouse the heart.

If these people had never been exposed to these appeals, there would have been some hope for them, but what hope can there be now, since, in having passed through them without permanent effect, they have become more hardened in the process than they were at first?

Here is a man dragged from an ice-pond, and brought into the infirmary. Hot flannels are at once applied, the limbs are chafed, every means known to modern science for restoring life is employed. At first it seems as if these appliances will take effect. There are twitchings and convulsive movements. But, alas! they soon subside, and the surgeon gravely shakes his head. "Can you do nothing else?" "Nothing," he replies. "I have used every method I can devise; and if these fail, it is impossible to renew again to life."

This passage has nothing to do with those who fear lest it condemns them. The presence of that anxiety, like the cry which betrayed the real mother in the days of Solomon, establishes beyond a doubt that you are not one that has fallen away beyond the possibility of renewal to repentance. If you are still touched by Gospel sermons, and are anxious to repent, and are in godly fear lest you should be a castaway, take heart! These are signs that this passage has no bearing on you. Why make yourself ill with a sick man's medicine?

But if you are growing callous and insensible under the preaching of the Gospel, look into this passage and see your doom, unless you speedily arrest your steps.

THE NATURAL ILLUSTRATION (verse 7). Behold that field, well situated, prepared by careful culture and arduous toil. The good seed is scattered with lavish hand, the rain comes oft upon it, the sunshine kisses it, the seasons, as they pass, woo it to bear fruit. At first it would appear as if it were about to answer the expectations freely entertained.

But see! The show of green which covers its face turns out to be a crop of briars and thorns. The owner for whom it was dressed comes to visit it. "What," cries he, "have you done all you could, this, and that, and the other?" "All," is the reply. Then the decision comes back, stern and sad, "It is useless to expend more time or care. Leave it to its fate. Let no fruit grow on it henceforth and forever."

We may resemble that field, and yet, whilst there is a spark of devotion, a thrill of holy longing, a sigh after a better life, a yearning to be penitent and holy, there is still hope. The great Husbandman will not cast us off, so long as there is one redeeming feature in our condition. He will not break the bruised reed, nor quench the smoking flax. He will not fail, nor be discouraged, until He has made the desert into a garden, and the wilderness like the paradise of God.

CHAPTER 15: THE ANCHORAGE OF THE SOUL

"Be followers of them who through faith and patience inherit the promises." (HEBREWS 6.12).

THE PROMISES OF GOD! That is a keyword here. Inherit the promises (verse 12). God made promise(verse 13). He obtained the promise (verse 15). The heirs of promise (verse 17).

But perhaps the reiteration of the word does not awaken the interest or stir the heart of those who read it. We are so familiar with it, and, above all, we are not in circumstances which make the divine promises specially precious. The night of sorrow must obscure our sky, or we can never descry or appreciate the stars of promise that sparkle as gems in the firmament of Scripture. Those who are rich and increased in goods and have need of nothing cannot realise what the promises of God really mean.

Possessed of a good income, guaranteeing the supply of every need, it is of little moment that God has pledged himself to provide all needful things for those who seek His kingdom first. Environed by troops of faithful friends, like so many successive lines of defence entrenched in the strong fortress of position and rank, there is less interest in the assurance that God will be the shield and buckler, the munition of rocks, the refuge from the storm for his saints.

But when riches dwindle, and friends fail, and health declines, and difficulty, persecution, and trial threaten, then the soul betakes itself to the promises of God, and ponders over them, studying them by the hour together, until it wakes up to find mines of treasure under pages which were blank as the moorlands beneath which coal-beds lie.

It would be well for some of us if God would strip us of all those things in which we place such confidence, so that we might be compelled, perhaps for the first time in our lives, to seek in Himself all that we are now wont to seek in His gifts. Oh, blessed loss, which should teach us our true wealth! Oh, happy deprivation, which should reveal our inexhaustible resources! Oh, loving discipline, which should break the cisterns that hold the brackish rainwater, and compel us to betake ourselves to the river of God, which proceeds from the throne of God and the Lamb!

The lax and cursory manner in which we read pages begemmed with divine promise is largely due to the fact that we have never been put into such straits of sorrow and privation as to appreciate their value. One crushing trial would open up whole tracts of promise, which are now like the shut doors of a corridor in a royal palace.

This is one reason why such a man as the Christian hero, Gordon, would spend hours over the Word of God, counting his Father's promises, holding them up as jewels in the sunshine, and rejoicing over them as great spoil. Such men as he have had little else. They have had no other resources to fall back on. They were driven to lay hold on them for very existence. And thus they fulfilled the enigma of the Apostle, "Having nothing, yet possessing all things." Those who are conscious of their poverty are they who become rich in faith, and heirs of the Kingdom.

It was in precisely such a condition that the Hebrews here addressed were found. Their goods had been spoiled, they had endured a great fight of affliction, they had been made a gazing stock both by reproaches and afflictions, all on which men are accustomed to rely had been swept from them. And therefore the Holy Spirit, in these pages, directs their minds to the exceeding great and precious promises, in which God pledged Himself to supply all their need, and to furnish from His own treasuries all, and more than all, that they had lost; not giving them these things in visible possession, but supplying them as they were needed, and in proportion to their faith. It was surely a good exchange, to lose all, and to recover all in God!

GOD'S PROMISES ARE RELIABLE. A good man's word is his bond. And when such a one has given a promise our anxiety is allayed, our fears are quieted, we have strong consolation. But if, in addition to the promise, our friend has solemnly bound himself by an oath, calling heaven and earth to witness, and God to ratify, the asseveration is so momentous, the appeal so awful, the impression made on the mind so deep, that, whatever happens, the soul shelters itself in the immutability of His decision. It is doubly impossible for Him to change or deceive. And this is the bond by which God has bound Himself.

When dealing with Abraham, God gave him repeated promises, first of the land, then of the seed, also of the blessing which should accrue to all generations of men through him. On one occasion He went through the form of covenant-making in vogue among the surrounding peoples (Genesis 15.7). But, on Mount Moriah, when the faithful patriarch had given the one stupendous evidence of faith and obedience, even to death, God swore, and "because He could swear by no greater, He swore by Himself." "By myself have I sworn, says the Lord', (Genesis 22.16).

And so it is with us. We who by faith are the spiritual seed of Abraham are blessed with him. "The promise is sure to all the seed. Not to that only which is of the law, but to that also which is of the faith of Abraham, who is the father of us all" (Romans 4.16). All the promises of God are Yes and Amen. He is not a man that He should lie, nor the son of man that He should repent.

He has well calculated His resources, before He has pledged Himself, and when once He has done so it is impossible that He should fail. Fall flat on the divine promises; cling to them as a shipwrecked sailor to the floating spar; venture all on them. Their fulfilment is guaranteed by covenant and oath; by blood and agony and death; by the light of the resurrection morning and the glory of the ascension mount; by the experience of myriads, who have never found them fail.

If any man living has found one promise untrustworthy, let him publish it to the world; and the heavens will clothe themselves in sackcloth, and the sun and moon and stars will reel from their seats, the universe will rock, and a hollow wind moan through creation, bearing the tidings that God is mutable, that God can lie. And that voice will be the herald of universal dissolution.

But it can never, never be. Heirs of promise! God's power is eternal, His counsel is immutable. Heaven and earth may pass away, but His word shall never pass away. You therefore may have strong consolation. Though you lose all else, your heritage in the word and oath of God shall be unimpaired, world without end.

GOD'S PROMISES, THUS ASSURED, MAKE AN ANCHORAGE FOR THE SOUL. Few things are more important for the mariner than to secure a good anchorage ground, where the soil will not give before the weight of the vessel and the strain of the storm. And with all those inclinations toward drifting which we have already considered, we urgently need to discover something permanent, unchanging, and satisfying, with which we may grapple by the anchor of our hope.

The faculty of hope in a Christian is not different to that of a worldly man. It is the same faculty or quality in each. But there is a vast difference in the ground in which the anchor is fixed. In the case of the worldly man, it is the loose, light, unreliable soil of peradventures and speculations. In the case of the Christian, it is the unyielding, immutable promise and oath of the Eternal God.

Therefore the former is often darkened with misgiving and fear, while the latter cries, without a shadow of doubt, "I know whom I have believed, and am persuaded."

Hope is something more than faith. Faith accepts and credits testimony; hope anticipates. Faith says the fruit is good, hope picks and eats. Faith is bud, hope blossom. Faith presents the cheque, hope lays out the amount received.

And such hope is the anchor of the soul. The comparison between hope and an anchor is familiar even to heathen writers, and it is easy to see how fit it is. It steadies the soul.

Take an illustration from common life. A young man pledges his troth to a poor but noble girl. He is drafted for foreign service, and says farewell for long years. Meanwhile she is left to do as well as she can to maintain herself. Work is scanty, wages low, she is sometimes severely tempted and tried. But, amidst all, she is kept true to her absent lover, and to her nobler self, by the little strand of hope which links her to a happy and united future.

So, when suffering or tempted or discouraged, our hope goes forward into the blessed future, depicted on the page of Scripture in glowing colours, and promised by the word of Him who cannot lie, and the anticipation of it fills the soul with courage and patience, so as to endure the trials of time, in view of the certain blessedness of eternity.

THE ANCHORAGE IN THE PROMISES HAS A THREEFOLD VALUE. It is sure, there is no fear of its failing. Sure as the sure mercies of David, sure as the "everlasting covenant, ordered in all things and sure"; sure as God can make it.

It is steadfast, its influence on the soul is to keep it steady: "Steadfast, unmoveable, always abounding in the work of the Lord." It enters into that within the veil. In the ancient world, when there was not water enough to float a ship into the harbour, a man would carry the anchor over the shoals, and fix it in the calm waters of the inner basin. In some such way as this, our Lord Jesus, when, like the high-priest in the Jewish Tabernacle, He passed through the blue veil that hides the celestial world from ours, took our hope with Him, and holds it there.

The Lord Jesus is our hope (1 Timothy 1.1 ; 1 John 3.3). He is our forerunner. He has preceded us into His Father's presence, the first fruits of them that slept. He has gone thither as our Representative and Priest.

When He majestically passed from the sight of His disciples, and was hidden from the eyes that longingly followed Him, He entered within the veil. There He ever lives, and because of it our hopes follow Him, centre in Him, and connect us already with that bright home of which He is the radiant centre.

THERE ARE CERTAIN QUALITIES WHICH WE MUST LEARN TO EXERCISE. Faith and patience can alone inherit the promises (verse 12). Abraham had patiently to endure before he received the promise (verse 15).

It is not easy to wait, or to let patience have her perfect work, and it is only possible to faith.

There is no sublimer instance of long waiting than the history of Abraham, for which his faith nerved him, and to whom the promise was literally fulfilled.

And so shall it be again. Patience weary, eager hearts. The time shall come when you shall lay hands on your capital. But be content in the meanwhile to enjoy the interest. The auspicious moment hastens when you shall know and taste all the blessedness of Paradise regained, but feast in the interim on the grapes of Eshcol, the pomegranates and other produce of the land.

Claim the patience of Christ, of which the last of the apostles, who had need of it to sustain him in the long delay, so sweetly speaks (Revelation 1.9). "Be you patient, establish your hearts, for the coming of the Lord draws nigh." "Let us run with patience the race set before us, looking unto Jesus." Thus shall we manifest "the patience of the saints"; and thus shall we, like those who have preceded us, finally inherit the promises.

CHAPTER 16: THE PRIESTHOOD OF CHRIST

"You are a Priest forever after the order of Melchizedek." (HEBREWS 7.17).

VARIOUS fancies have gathered around the person of Melchizedek, investing him with extraordinary qualities, but it is better far to think of him simply as the head or chieftain of a large family or clan, which gathered around the site to be known, in after years, as "the holy city." Already its name was shadowed forth in the term "Salem," which designated the clustered rude huts or tents. Amid the almost universal lawlessness and depravity which swept over Palestine, righteousness and peace seem to have fled for shelter to this little community, where alone due reverence was given to the Most High God, possessor of heaven and earth.

How this oasis had come into existence amid the surrounding moral desert we cannot tell, but it may have been due to the commanding personal influence of the king, who, according to patriarchal custom, as father of the family, was not only the ruler of the family life, but leader in the family devotions. And thus, while Melchizedek was king of Salem, he was also priest of the Most High.

Moreover, it would appear that he bore a special commission, and was raised up for a specific purpose, as the ordained messenger between God and men, and as embodying a striking portraiture of the priesthood to be exercised for man by the Son of God.

Note the significance of the words, made like to the Son of God (verse 3). Christ's eternal Priesthood was the archetypal reality, after the similitude of which that of Melchizedek was fashioned. It was as if the Father could not await the day of His Son's priestly entrance within the veil but must needs anticipate the marvels of His ministry by embodying its leading features in miniature. Let us now study some of them.

CHRIST IS KING AS WELL AS PRIEST (verse 1). History gives its unanimous judgment against the temporal and the spiritual power being vested in the same man. In Israel the two offices were kept rigorously separate, and when, on one occasion, a king passed the sacred barrier, and, snatching up a censer, strode into the inner court, he was at once followed by the remonstrances of the priestly band, whilst the white brand of leprosy wrote his doom upon his brow; "and he himself hastened to go out, because the Lord had smitten him."

But the simple monarch of whom we write, living before gathering abuses forbade the union, combined in his person the royal sceptre and the sacerdotal censer. And herein he foreshadowed the Christ.

Jesus is King and Priest. He is King because He is a priest. He is highly exalted, demanding homage from every knee, and confession from every lip, because He became obedient to the death of the cross. He bases His royal claims, not on hereditary descent, though the blood of David flowed in His veins; not on conquest or superior force; not on the legislation that underpins the kingdom of heaven among men: but on this, that He redeemed us to God by His blood.

He is the King of glory, because He is the Lamb of God which takes away the sin of the world. The cross was the steppingstone to His throne.

And He cannot fulfil His office as Priest unless He be first recognised as King. Many fail to derive all the blessing offered to men through the Priesthood of Christ, because they are not willing to admit his claims as King. They do not reverence and obey Him. They do not open the whole of the inner realm to His sceptre.

They endeavour to serve two masters, and to stand well with empires as different as light and darkness, heaven and hell, God and Satan. There must be consecration before there can be perfect faith, coronation before deliverance, the King before the Priest.

The order is invariable. First King of Righteousness, and after that also King of Peace (verse 2). " Peace, give us peace!" is the importunate demand of men. Peace at any price, by all means peace.

But God, in the deep waters, lays the foundation of righteousness; "and the work of righteousness shall be peace, and the effect of righteousness quietness and assurance forever." It is of no use to heal the wound slightly, saying, "Peace, peace," when there is none. Infinitely better is it to probe to the bottom, and to build up from a sound and healthy foundation to the surface of the flesh.

And the King of Peace will never enter your soul until you have first acknowledged Him as King of Righteousness, submitting yourself to His righteous claims, and renouncing the righteousness which is of the law for that which is by faith.

It is lamentable to find how few Christians, comparatively, are realising the full meaning or power of Christianity. Joyless, fruitless, powerless, they are a stumbling block to the world, and a mockery to devils.

And is not the reason here? They are not right. They are harbouring traitors and aliens in their souls. They constantly condemn themselves in things that they allow.

No doubt they excuse themselves, and invent special reasons to palliate their faults, so that what would be inadmissible with others is pardonable in them. What special pleading! What ingenious arguments! What gymnastic feats are theirs! But all in vain. Let any such who read these lines learn that it is vitally necessary to make Christ King, and King of Righteousness, before ever they can appreciate the peace which accrues from His Priesthood on our behalf.

CHRIST'S PRIESTHOOD WAS NOT INHERITED (verse 3). This also comes out clearly in the history of the priest-king of Salem.

The Levitical priest had carefully to trace his connection with Aaron, and hence the elaborate genealogies of which some parts of the Bible are full. The priests, at the time of the return from Babylon, who could not prove their pedigree, were suspended until a priest arose with Urim and Thummim. But Melchizedek's priesthood had evidently nothing to do with his descent. He was independent of priestly pedigree.

Of course it is not necessary to infer that he really had no human parentage and that he knew neither birth nor death. This is neither stated nor assumed. The argument is simply built on the omission of any reference to these events in ordinary human life; and aims to prove that, therefore, this old-world priesthood was quite independent of those conditions which were of prime importance in the Levitical dispensation. It was of an entirely different order from that which officiated in the Jewish Temple, and was, therefore, so capable to represent Christ's.

As God, our Lord had no mother. As man, no father. He did not Spring from a family of priests, for it is evident that our Lord sprang out of Judah, of which tribe Moses spoke nothing concerning the priesthood.

What was allegorically true of Melchizedek was literally true of Jesus, who has had neither beginning of days nor end of life. His Priesthood, therefore, is utterly unique. He stands amongst men unrivalled. There have been none like Him before nor since. His functions derived from none, shared by none, transmitted to none. Made what He was from all eternity by the foreknowledge and counsel of God.

There never was a beginning to the priestliness of our Saviour's heart. There is no date in heaven's calendar for the uprising within Him of mercy and pity, and of the intention to stand as the Advocate and Intercessor for our race. Before the mountains were brought forth, or the heavens and earth were made, there was already in His thoughts the germ of that marvellous drama which is slowly unfolding before the gaze of the universe. He was Priest, as well as the Lamb slain, from before the foundation of the world.

Love is eternal. Sacrifice is one of the root principles of the being of God. Priesthood is part of the texture of the nature of the Second Person in the adorable Trinity. There need be no fear, therefore, that He will ever desert His office, or lay it aside for some other purpose, or cease to have compassion on the ignorant and erring, the tempted and fallen.

CHRIST'S PRIESTHOOD IS CONTINUAL (verse 3). The priests of Aaron's line were not suffered to continue by reason of death. But of Him "it is witnessed that He lives" (verse 8).

Hallelujah! a Priest has arisen "after the power of an endless life" (verse 16). "The Lord swore and will not repent, You are a Priest forever" (verse 21). "Because He abides forever, His Priesthood is unchangeable" (verse 24). "He ever lives to make intercession" (verse 25). "Consecrated forevermore" (verse 28).

What explicit and abundant testimony! Our High-Priest shall never ascend Mount Hor to be stripped of His robes of office and die. The secrets confided to Him need never be told again to His successor. The tender love which links Him and us shall never be snapped or cut in death. No one else will ever be called in to take His place in the superintendence of our souls.

This teaching rebukes two errors. (1) The error of those who teach sinlessness in the flesh. It is impossible to exaggerate the mischief which is being wrought just now by some who take advantage of the universal yearning for a higher experience, and are holding out to credulous souls the prospect of reaching a position in which they will no longer need to confess sin, no longer require perpetual cleansing in the blood of Christ, no longer be sensible of their sinnership.

They who speak thus confound sin and sins. They apply the term infirmity to acts and dispositions which the Word of God calls by blacker, darker names. This teaching lowers a man's standard of sin to suit the erroneous doctrine which he has imbibed.

It is contrary to the distinct teaching of Scripture that the flesh in the believer may yet lust for the upper hand. It is in Opposition to all deeper experience of the Christian life, which goes to show that, even when we know nothing against ourselves, yet are we not hereby justified, because there may be many evils of which, for want of clearer light, we are completely ignorant, but which stand out patent enough to the eye of Him who judges us, the Lord who searches the heart and reins.

The error of those who teach the perplexity of a sacrificing priesthood. Of course all believers are priests, in the sense of offering the sacrifice of praise and prayer, the offerings of self-denying love. But there are many among us who persist in affirming that they are called, in addition, constantly to offer the perpetual sacrifice of Calvary, in the elements of the Lord's Supper.

Amid the ceremonial of the mass, as offered in too many of our English churches by professed Protestants, claiming to be priests, it is hard to see any trace of the simple institution of the Lord's Supper. And it makes one tingle with righteous indignation to see the way in which these blind leaders of the blind are deceiving the multitudes to the ruin of their soul.

Sometimes one longs for the withering sarcasm of an Erasmus, the sturdy common sense of a Latimer, the vehemence of a Knox, to show up the unscriptural pretensions of these men, tricked out in the gaudy finery of pagan costumes, and going through mummeries which would provoke to laughter, if the whole system were not so inexpressibly sad. "How long, 0 Lord, how long!"

But, after all, the true way to meet these errors is to insist upon our Lord's continual and unchangeable intercession and priesthood. Surely if He lives and continues His work, it is a piece of impertinent and arrogant folly to intrude upon His functions. We must revert to the earlier methods of Scriptural interpretation and exposition before ever we shall be able to forearm our young people against the monstrous errors of our times, or win back those who have been so disastrously led astray.

CHAPTER 17: THE SUPERLATIVE GREATNESS OF CHRIST

"Able to save them to the uttermost that come unto God by Him, seeing He ever lives to make intercession for them." (HEBREWS 7.25).

THIS chapter needs to be read under a deep sense of sin, to be properly understood and appreciated. It is the conscious sinner who needs the Priest.

We can do very well with Christ as Teacher, Philanthropist, Ideal Man, until we see ourselves as we are in the sight of God, but when that vision is given to us, our hearts cry out with an exceeding great and bitter cry for the Priest, who can stand for us with God, and for God with us.

There is urgent need for a fresh consciousness and conviction of our sinnership, both amongst unbelievers and professing Christians. Light views of sin give slight views of the sacrifice of Calvary, of the need for propitiation, and of the dread future penalty on wilful wrongdoing.

Did men really understand what sin is, they would not talk so glibly of their complete deliverance from it, confounding as they do the few sins of which they are cognisant with the mass of evil that lies still in their nature, like the mud at the bottom of a pellucid lake, only needing to be stirred to show itself.

And if men really felt their sins, there would be a unanimous rush to the precious Blood and to the only priest for absolution and pardon.

It is hardly likely that these poor words can affect the set of the current, yet, if it were possible to reach the great mass of the preachers of the present day, one would urge them to lay aside their literary essays, their arguments with evolutionists, their poetry and rhetoric, and to bring the trenchant teaching of God's Word to bear on human consciences and lives.

Let them attack sin as sin. Let them deal with the sins of their congregations specifically, as the sniper marks his man for his bullet. Let them show what God thinks of the sins which we treat so lightly. And as soon as we get back to the old fashioned style of preaching, we shall see a revival of old fashioned conversions.

It is of no use complaining, when we are ourselves to blame. Human nature is unaltered. The law of God is unchanged. The cry of the conscience is stifled, not silenced. Again shall we hear of multitudes pierced to the heart, and crying for mercy. And then the Priesthood of Christ, as described here, will acquire a new preciousness.

HE IS A GREAT HIGH-PRIEST (verse 4). How great appears from the episode here referred to. Flushed with victory, bringing with him all the captives and goods which Chedorlaomer had swept away from Sodom, the patriarch Abraham had nearly reached his own camp.

But as he drew nigh to Salem, where peace and righteousness dwelt beneath the rule of Melchizedek, he was met by this saintly figure, bearing in his hands the sacred emblems of bread and wine: meet type of Him who often accosts us on the road of life, when weary with conflict, or when entering into subtle temptation, and refreshes us with the bread of His flesh, and the wine of His blood. And Abraham received a blessing at his hand, and gave him tithes of all (Genesis 14.19, 20).

Does not this prove the greatness of Melchizedek? The Levites and priests were indeed permitted to take tithes of their brethren, but this glorious priest feels no compunction to take tithes of one of another race. He rose above the narrow boundaries of race or blood, and was prepared to do his office with equal care for an alien as for his own.

This unsectarian, cosmopolitan, large-hearted view of his obligations to man as man is a true mark of greatness. And in this he manifests a trait of the greatness of our dear Lord, whose Priesthood overleaps the limits which might be set by nationality or birth, and deals with man as man; with you, reader, and me, if only we will come to Him.

Besides this, since the greater must bless the less, it is obvious that Abraham, great and good though he was, the friend of God, and the recipient of the promises, must have felt that Melchizedek was his superior, or he would never have treated him with such marked respect (Hebrews 7.6, 7). Surely, then, this holy man was a fit representative of our blessed Lord, to whom all the noblest in heaven and earth bow the knee, confessing that He is Lord, and consecrating to Him, not a tenth only, but the whole of what they have and are.

HE IS A GREATER HIGH-PRIEST THAN AARON OR HIS SONS. When Abraham knelt beneath that royal and priestly hand, he did not do so for himself alone, but as a representative man. First and head of his race, his descendants were identified with him in his deed. Levi, therefore, who receives tithes, paid tithes in the patriarch, and, in doing so, forevermore took up the second place as inferior, and second best.

"Stop," cries an objector; "if you affirm this inferiority of the Jewish priesthood to that of Melchizedek, you are making an assertion so far-reaching in its results as to need some further corroboration. Are you quite sure that this is as you say?"

"Certainly," is the reply; "else, why should there be so emphatic an announcement made in David's Psalms of the coming of another Priest long after the Jewish priesthood had been in operation?

If perfection were by the Levitical priesthood, what further need was there that another Priest should arise after the order of Melchizedek and not be called after the order of Aaron?

"But stay," again interposes the objector; "if you are going to supersede the Levitical priesthood, you are of necessity making a change in all that ceremonial law which rested on the priesthood as an arch upon its keystone. Are you prepared to sweep away a system so venerable, so religiously maintained, the bulwark of religion, the institution of God?"

"I am prepared for this," is the reply. "The previous commandments that relate to sacrifices and rites and ceremonies will have to go. They were temporary and imperfect. Types, not realities, moulds, not the real vessels, shadows, not the substance. They made nothing perfect. Their office was to bring in a better hope, but, now that this is come, they may be annulled and laid aside."

It seems a light thing to us, but it was of the gravest import to those who were here addressed. To them the Jewish priesthood and ceremonial were more than a state religion, they were religion itself. Tradition, custom, ancestral veneration, personal admiration, and adherence, all these ties had to be rudely snapped, as they were compelled to admit the cogency of this inspired and irresistible argument.

If Jesus were indeed the Priest spoken of by David in Psalm 110 - and of this there seemed no doubt because it was so often applied to Him (Matthew 22.44; Acts 2.34) - then there could be no doubt that His Priesthood was better than Aaron's, and that the whole system of which the Levitical priesthood was the essential characteristic must pass away before that system which gathers around the person and work of the Lord Jesus.

We must distinguish between the moral and the ceremonial law. The latter is transient, and was fulfilled in Jesus Christ; the former, of course, is of permanent and eternal force, written on the conscience of man and the government of the world.

We can only stay for a moment here to show how absurd it is for either the Roman or the Anglican priest to base his pretensions on the example of the Old Testament. To do so is to confess their inferiority to the only Priesthood which is recognised in the present age. They are in evil case.

Press them for their warrant of existence. If they quote Revelation 1.6, then we all have an equal right to wear their dress and fulfil their office. If they quote Leviticus, then are they hopelessly undone, for that priesthood has been superseded. The time is coming when all his people will have to disavow connection with those men whose pretensions are baseless, or worse, delusive, and an unwarrantable intrusion into the sacred offices of Christ. Alas the poor souls, deluded and fleeced by them!

HE IS THE GREATEST OF HIGH-PRIESTS. Because He was made priest by the oath of God (verses 20, 21). Ordinary priests had no such sanction to their appointment, but He by an oath. Jehovah swore, and will not change His mind. His appointment is final, absolute, immutable. It never can be superseded, as that of Aaron has been. Heaven and earth may pass away, but it will not pass away.

Because He continues ever. His is the Priesthood in which throbs the power of an endless life (verse 16). It is witnessed of Him, that He lives. "Behold," said He, "I am alive forevermore."

What a contrast to all human priests, on whose graves this epitaph may ever be inscribed, "Not suffered to continue by reason of death." One by one they grow old and die, the eye, often filmed with tears, is closed, the heart stands still, the hands, often raised in absolution, crossed meekly on the breast, as if asking for pardon.

But He ever lives. And of this perpetual life there are two blessed results. On the one hand, He has an untransferable Priesthood (verse 24), on the other hand, He is able to save them to the uttermost that come unto God by Him (verse 25).

There is no limit to His salvation, no barrier beyond which He may not pass. Uttermost in time, and in character, and in desperation, you may be at one of the ends of the earth, yet you shall be lifted to the uttermost degree of glory.

To the uttermost - from sins of thought as well as of word and deed, to the uttermost, in cleansing the thoughts and intents of the heart.

Because of His blameless character. Holy towards God; harmless towards man, undefiled in heart, separate from sinners in life. Not needing to offer up sacrifice for Himself, as the priests did always before offering for the congregation, not requiring to make a daily or yearly repetition of that perfect sacrifice and oblation which was once made on the cross (verses 26, 27).

Because of the dignity of His Person (verse 28). The office of mediation is no longer entrusted to a man, or set of men, encompassed by infirmities. See! through the shining ranks of being there advances the Son, Light of Light, Fellow of Yahweh, Co-equal with God, One with Father and Spirit in the ever-blessed Trinity. He is solemnly consecrated to this task of reconciling and saving sinners. All heaven hears and ratifies the oath.

And surely we may well ponder what must be our worth in the thought of God, and what our destiny, when our case is undertaken, amid such solemnities, by One so august, so glorious, so divine, as the High-Priest, who now awaits the appeal of the humblest penitent of the human race. "Such a High-Priest became us."

"TO THE UTTERMOST." Eyes may light on these words, weary with weeping, of those who have been reduced well-nigh to despair through the greatness and virulence of their sins. Not only does the record of the past seem too black to be forgiven, but old habits are perpetually reasserting themselves; ridiculing the most steadfast resolutions, and smiting the inner life of the soul down to the ground.

At such times we are disposed to envy the vegetable and animal creation, which are not capable of sin, or the myriads of sweet children who have been taken home to God before the time of conscious rebellion and war could rend their infant hearts.

But the greatness of our sin is always less than the greatness of God's grace. Where the one abounds, the other much more abounds. If we go down to the bottoms of the mountains and touch the heart of the deep, deeper than all is the redeeming mercy of God. The love and grace and power of Jesus are more than our unutterable necessities.

Only trust Him, He is "able to save unto the uttermost", and He is as willing as able.

There are many in these days filled with questionings about the clean heart, the extent to which we may be delivered from sin, and such like speculations. To these we say, Cease to think of cleansing, and consider the Cleanser, forbear to speculate on the deliverance, and deal with the Deliverer, be not so eager as to the nature of the salvation, but let the Saviour into your heart, and be sure that so long as He is in possession, He will exert so salutary an effect, that sin, however mighty, shall instantly lose its power over the tempest-driven soul that comes through Him to God, the source of holiness.

CHAPTER 18: THE TRUE TABERNACLE

"According to the pattern showed to you in the mount." (HEBREWS 8.5).

THERE were three stages by which Moses, the man of God, ascended into the Mount. To the first, he went in company with Aaron, Nadab, and Abihu, and seventy elders of the children of Israel, the chosen representatives of the people. "And they saw the God of Israel, and there was under His feet as it were a paved work of a sapphire stone, and as it were the body of heaven in its clearness. They saw God, and did eat and drink" (Exodus 24.10, 11).

This eating and drinking was evidently a symbol of friendship and peace, based upon the shedding of the blood, which is recorded in the previous verses. We, too, may see God, and eat of the flesh and drink of the blood of the Son of Man, on the basis of that precious blood by which we have been made nigh.

When this feast was over, the voice of God called Moses up to a higher range, a further steep. He first bade the elders tarry where they were, and then, accompanied only by Joshua, he rose up, and went into the mount of God, on which the cloud brooded, steeped and bathed in the glory of the Lord, like the long bars of cloud in the brilliance of a setting sun.

But on the seventh day, even Joshua was left behind. God called to Moses out of the cloud. And Moses went up further into the mount, deeper and yet deeper into the heart of the burning glory. All his senses were keenly awake to the scenes around him, and entranced, each the channel for tides of rapturous enjoyment, without pain, without self-consciousness, without the paralysis of fear, as if one were borne ever onward by a tide of glory and music, each movement of which was rapture. "And Moses was in the Mount forty days and forty nights."

During that time minute instructions were given Moses concerning the Tabernacle, which was to be erected on the plains below. Those instructions are given in Exodus 25; 26; 27, and are exceedingly minute. But nothing was left to human fancy. Beginning with the ark and its mercy-seat as the throne of God, the instructions pass through the table of shittim wood, the candlestick with its seven branches, the boards and curtains and hangings, until they end at the great brazen altar in the court of the Tabernacle, where God and the sinner met.

Is not this also the path trodden by the Lord Himself, the substance of all these types, Who came from the bosom of the Father to the cross of Calvary, the brazen altar where He put away the sins of men?

But, in addition to the minute description thus given, there appears to have been presented to the mind of Moses some representation of the things which he was bidden to construct. It was as if the eternal realities which had dwelt forever in the mind of God took some visible shape before his vision. The unseen became visible. The eternal took form. A pattern was shown him. He trod the aisles of the true Tabernacle. He beheld the heavenly things themselves. And it was after this pattern that he was repeatedly urged and commanded to build. "According to all that I show you, after the pattern of the Tabernacle, and the pattern of all the instruments thereof, even so shall you make it" (Exodus 25.9, 40; 26.30; 27.8).

THE JEWISH RITUAL DESERVES DEVOUT STUDY. It is always interesting to study methods of religious worship, even though the rites have become obsolete, the altars deserted, and the dust of priest and votary has long since mingled in the sand of the desert or the verdure of the glade.

Who can look unmoved at the gigantic monuments which rear themselves in the dense forests of Central Mexico, the remnants of an age of giants who have passed away, giving no clue to the symbols or hieroglyphs which they have carved? Who can walk unmoved through the stone circles of Stonehenge, Keswick, or Penmaenmawr, and not fall into pensive musings?

For this reason, if for no other, the Levitical ritual would ever be possessed of intrinsic interest. When we think of the noble spirits who have bequeathed us our most precious religious records, who sang in the Psalms, and wept in the Lamentations, and flashed with the ecstasy of Messianic prediction and prophecy; and all of whom were trained in the system of which the Tabernacle was the focus and heart, we cannot fail to examine it with holy and reverent curiosity, as if one should visit the nursery or schoolhouse where loved and honoured teachers spent their earliest years.

But there is a yet deeper interest here. For we are told that these things were made after the pattern of things in the heavens. Every knob, and tache, and curtain, and vessel, and piece of furniture, had some analogue, some spiritual counterpart of which it was the rude and material expression. Through these examples and shadows there is no doubt that the ancient saints caught glimpses of the eternal realities.

We infer this, because there is such a similarity between their religious life, as expressed in their writings, and our own. But if they, who had nothing but the type to guide them, were able to discern so many deep and holy lessons through its medium, how much more evidently should we be able to see the grand principles of redemption in the ancient ritual, when before us have passed the scenes of Bethlehem, Calvary, the Garden of Arimathea, and the Ascension Mount!

Sometimes in a shadow we may see details of workmanship which otherwise in the substance we might have missed. One of the most wonderful achievements of the present day is sun-photography, by which photographs are obtained of the sun-disk under certain conditions. And it is obviously much easier to investigate the nature of the sun from such photographs than to study it amid the unbearable glory of its presence. The eye may quietly pursue its investigations undazzled and unabashed.

So we may better understand some of the details of Christ's work, as we study Leviticus, than when we stand with the apostles amid the marvels of the cross, or with the Seer amid the supernal blaze of Apocalyptic vision.

Turn not lightly then from the Book of Leviticus, which shadows forth the Gospel, and, indeed, gives much of the terminology, the phrases and symbols, to be afterward employed. Beneath the teaching of the same Holy Spirit as taught Moses of old we explore the sacred meanings which underlie ark and propitiatory; fine twined linen and blue, candlestick and table, altar of incense and altar of burnt-offering, basin and vessel and snuffer. Each is like a hook in the divine household, to which God has attached a sacred meaning, and which will yield up its secret to those who reverently ask and seek and knock.

Adapting some memorable words, we may say: "The invisible things of God, from the construction of the Tabernacle, are clearly seen, being understood by the things that were made, even His eternal purpose of redemption."

THE TRUTHS OF THE GOSPEL ARE ETERNAL REALITIES. We must not think that they are ever destined to pass away, as the Jewish types did. They cannot. They are the heavenly things themselves. They are the true, the ideal, the divine. They have always been what they are. They always will be what they are.

We may yet have to see much deeper into them, we may need to be taught them in yet higher methods of divine communication. We may have to be lifted on to a loftier region of experience in order to comprehend them. But they are essentially and forever settled, the granite of eternal fact. Any structure built on them shall last forever. The Jews had only the example, we have the reality; they the picture, we the person; they the shadow, we the substance.

It is interesting to feel that Moses saw no other truth in God's revelation than what Paul saw; though to Moses it shaped itself in the Tabernacle with its layers of skins, whilst to Paul it took shape in glowing trains of splendid argument and rhetoric. But ever in the mind and thought of God there has been the same distinction between holiness and sin, ever the need of sacrifice, even unto death, ever the demand for shed life, as the only means through which the sinner may approach His holy Majesty; ever the requirements of the incense of praise, the bread of obedience, the light of an illuminated character; ever the priest to make intercession, and ever the aisles and courts and spaces dedicated to worship and intercourse, lofty as the fellowship between the Father and the Son.

Calvary is no novelty, nor the Priesthood, nor the work of Jesus. They represent the shining forth of eternal facts in the deepest nature of God. To ignore them is to miss union with God on the most fundamental laws and processes of His being. The Lamb was slain before the foundation of the world, and He appears in heaven still bearing the marks of His death, "a Lamb as it had been slain."

OUR PLACE OF WORSHIP. We must needs assemble ourselves in places of assembly with fellow Christians, but in point of fact not one of them is essential to true worship. The type has passed, and we know that the Jewish Tabernacle is no more. But what do we see? Men are trying to reproduce it, or to invent a substitute for it.

Ah, how greatly they misconceive our true position! We certainly neither need the Jewish Tabernacle nor any substitute; because we are constituted priests of the heavenly tabernacle, which no human hand ever reared, and which is the meeting place between God and all true hearts, yea, of all who love God. "Neither in this mountain, nor yet at Jerusalem, shall you worship the Father."

When we meet a company of our fellow Christians, we are not to think of them as the whole of those with whom we worship. The true worshipper is one of a great festal throng, which is filling the spiritual temple. We are but part of a congregation consisting of all the sainted dead, and the believing living, in all communions, and throughout the universe of God. The prisoner, the traveller, the invalid, the mother, the nurse - all meet there in unison, and worship God together. All are priests, and yonder is the High-Priest, who has passed through the heavens and ever lives to make intercession.

"A minister of the true tabernacle." How ridiculous do those appear to such an assembly who arrogate to themselves priestly pretensions, and who would make us believe that they are repeating the sacrifice of Christ! In this temple at least they are not wanted, for Christ is here to offer the sacrifice Himself.

THE TRUE PATTERN OF OUR LIFE IS SUGGESTED HERE. We have many plans and schemes and patterns, but how often abortive and disappointing! Would that we could spend long periods with God in the mount, getting His pattern of our life and work! There is nothing higher for us than to build up some resemblance to God's eternal thought. All structures built on that scheme will stand forever. And God will ever find material, more than enough, for those who dare to be singular, because they are true to the pattern which He shows on the mount.

And if it be asked what that pattern is which God will show us in the mount of communion, we may reply: it is the life and character and work of Jesus Christ our Lord, the model and exemplar and pattern of all that is true and just and pure and lovely and of good report. See that you make your life on this pattern, which God waits to show you in the mount. God calls you to it, and He will enable you to perform.

CHAPTER 19: THE TWO COVENANTS

"I will be to them a God, and they shall be to me a people." (HEBREWS 8.10).

A NEW word comes into this marvellous treatise which may repel some, as having a theological sound, and yet it contains new depths of meaning and interest for us all. It is the word Covenant.

We all understand pretty clearly the covenants into which men enter with each other with respect to property, or other matters of daily business. One man undertakes to do certain things, on condition that another pledges himself to do certain other things. When these respective undertakings are settled, they are engrossed on parchment, signed, and sealed, and from that moment each party is honourably bound to perform his share in the transaction.

In some such way, adapting Himself to our methods of thought and practice, the eternal God has entered into covenant with faithful and obedient souls. Nor is it possible to overestimate the condescension on His part, or the honour and advantage placed within our reach, by such relationship. It seems too wonderful to be true. Yet it must be true, for on no other grounds than its revealed truthfulness could it ever have become a matter of human statement or debate.

The covenant between a prince and a beggar, or between a man like William Penn and the American Indians, is dwarfed into utter insignificance and paltriness when mentioned in the same day as the covenant between God and the soul of man.

Theologians have detected several different kinds of covenant in the course of human history, and as depicted in the Bible. But it is sufficient for us to notice the two covenants, Old and New, mentioned in this paragraph.

And the basis of the whole argument is contained in Jeremiah 31.31-34, in which there is a distinction made between the covenant made with the fathers - when God took them out of the land of Egypt, - and that new covenant, which in the days of Jeremiah, was still future. Moses was the mediator of the first, as Jesus is of the second.

THE MOSAIC COVENANT. It was often reiterated in very gracious and searching tones. Take, for instance, that scene which took place as the vast host defiled into the plain beneath the brow of Sinai, in the third month of the Exodus. As yet there was no cloud or fire on Sinai's crest, but a proposition was made to the people by Moses, that if they, on their side, would obey God's voice and keep His word, God, on His side, would do two things. He would regard them as His own peculiar treasure above all people, and He would take them to Himself as a kingdom of priests, and a holy nation (Exodus 19.5, 6). And the people, little counting the cost, or realising all that was involved, cried with one glib, unanimous voice, "All that the Lord has spoken will we do." They thus entered into covenant.

Shortly after, when the Ten Commandments had been given, the terms of the covenant on God's part were very much enlarged. On the fulfilment, on the part of the people, of the old condition of obedience, God went further than ever before in His promises, which comprehended a vast variety of need, and consisted of many parts (Exodus 23.22-31). And again the people gave one mighty, unanimous shout of assent (24.3).

Nor was this all, for when, with the intention of recording these solemn engagements, they were entered in the Book of the Covenant, and read publicly amid the solemn ratification of sprinkled blood, the people again said, "All that the Lord has said will we do, and be obedient" (Exodus 24.7).

But how little they knew themselves! Within a week or two they were dancing wildly around the golden calf, and within a few months there was not one who dared affirm that he had kept the covenant in every jot and tittle. Nay, on the contrary: "which my covenant they brake, says the Lord."

What else could be expected of them! Although Moses did write them a second and detailed statement of the conditions of the covenant in the Book of Deuteronomy, with the reiterated demand, that occurs like a refrain, "You shall observe to do."

There were two great defects in that old covenant, which arose out of the weakness of poor human nature. In the first place, it gave no power, no moral dynamics, to enable the human covenanters to do what they promised, and, secondly, it could not provide for the effectual putting away of those sins which arose from their failure to carry into effect their covenanted vows (Hebrews 9.9).

Surely the majority of men, aiming after a religious life, pass through an experience like this. When first we are redeemed by the blood of the Lamb, and brought out into the new life, we seem to stand again under Mount Sinai, or, better still, our conscience becomes our Sinai, and from its highest point we seem to hear the voice of God, engaging Himself to be a God to us if we will in all things obey His voice. And this we immediately pledge ourselves to do.

We are not insincere, we really mean to perform it; we are enamoured at the ideal of life presented to us. It is not only desirable as the condition of blessings, but it is eminently attractive and lovely.

But we make a profound mistake in pledging ourselves, for we are undertaking a matter which is totally beyond our reach. As well might a paralysed man undertake to climb Mount Blanc, or a bankrupt to pay his debts.

We soon learn that sin has paralysed all our moral motor nerves. The good we would, we do not: the evil we would not, we do. We are brought into captivity to the law of sin in our members, which wars against the law of our mind. We go out to shake ourselves, as at other times, but we fail to realise that razors have passed over our locks of strength, leaving us powerless and helpless.

It seems a pity that each has to learn the uselessness of these attempts for himself, instead of profiting by the experience of others and the records of the past. Yet so it is. One after another starts to earn the privilege of God's presence and smile and blessing by being good and obedient and punctilious in complying with rules and forms and regulations. It goes on well for a little while, but soon utterly breaks down. We are baffled and beaten, as sea-fowl who dash themselves against a lighthouse tower in the storm, and then fall wounded into the yeasty foam beneath.

We are slow to learn that, as we receive justification, so must we receive sanctification, from the hands of God as His free gift.

If any reader of these lines is trying to keep up a friendly relationship with God on this principle of try and do and keep, the sooner that soul realises the certainty of failure, not for want of will, but through the weakness of the moral nature, and yields itself to the grace revealed in the second and better covenant, the more quickly will it find a secure and happy resting place, from which it will not be disturbed or driven, world without end.

THE BETTER COVENANT. It is so much better than that of Moses in this way. It pledges God to even better promises (verse 6) than those of the earlier covenant, promises which for a moment demand our attention, and there is no pledge or undertaking of any kind demanded from us. There are no ifs, no injunctions of 'observe to do', no conditions of obedience to be fulfilled. From first to last it consists of the 'I wills' of the Most High. Count them up in this marvellous enumeration (verse 10; 2.12), and then dare to claim that each should be fulfilled in your personal experience because this is the covenant under which we are living, and through which we have access to God.

"I will write my laws into their minds". That refers to the intellectual faculty, which thinks, remembers, argues. It will be of inestimable value to have them there for constant reference, so that they shall always stand inscribed on the side posts and lintels of the inner life, demanding reverence, and compelling daily attention.

"I will write them upon their hearts." That is the seat of the emotional life and of the affections. If they are written there, they must engage our love. And what a man loves, he is pretty certain to follow and obey.

"A little lower," said the dying veteran, as they probed for the bullet, which had sunk deep down into his breast, "and you will find the Emperor", and in the case of the Christian who has been taken into covenant with God, the law is inscribed on the deepest affections of his being. He obeys because he loves to obey. He stays in his Master's service, not because he must, but because he chooses it for himself, saying, as his ear is bored to the door, "I love my Master, I will not go out free."

"I will be to them a God, and they shall be to me a people." The last clause is even better than the first, because it implies the keeping power of God. His chosen people so wandered from Him that He once called them "LoAmmi" Not my people (Hosea 1). But if we are ever to be His people, people for His own possession then it can only result from the operation of His gracious Spirit, who keeps us, as the sun restrains the planets from dashing off into space to become wandering stars.

"All shall know me." Oh, rapture of raptures! can it be? To know God! To know the deep things of God. To know Him, or to be known of Him. To know Him as Abraham did, to whom He told His secrets, as Moses did, who conversed with Him face to face, or as the Apostle John did, when he beheld Him in the visions of the Apocalypse. And that this privilege should be within reach of the least!

"I will be merciful to their unrighteousness." In the old covenant there was little room for mercy. It was a matter of voluntary agreement; if one of the covenanting parties failed in the least particular, there was no obligation on the other to remain faithful to their mutual agreement. The failure of one party neutralised the whole covenant. But there is no such stringency here. On the contrary, mercy is admitted into the relationship, and exercises her gracious sway.

"I will remember their sins and iniquities no more." As a score is forgotten when blotted from a slate, so shall sin be, as if obliterated from the memory of God. It will be forgotten, as a debt paid years ago. It will be so entirely put out of mind that it shall be as if it had never been. If sought for, not found. The handwriting nailed through. The stone dropped into ocean depths. The cloud absorbed by the summer heat, as it fades from the deep blue sky.

Joseph's brethren, in their last approach to Joseph, after their father's death, betrayed a fear that though his resentment was cloaked, it was not thoroughly relinquished. But their fears were entirely groundless. They discovered that the offence had utterly passed from their brother's thought, and Joseph wept when they spoke to him. In some such way as this God ceases to consider our sins, and grieves if we do not believe the thoroughness of His abundant pardon.

Are you enjoying the terms of this covenant in your daily experience? God is prepared to fulfil them to the letter. Count on Him to do as He has promised. Reckon on His faithfulness. Claim that each pledge shall be realised in you to the fullest limits of His wealth, and your need.

Do not try to invent conditions or terms not laid down by Him, but gladly accept the position of doing nothing to earn or win, and of accepting all that God gives, without money and without price.

Do you ask how God can call this a covenant, in which there is no second covenanting party? The answer is easy. Jesus Christ has stood in our stead, and has not only negotiated this covenant, but has fulfilled in our name, and on our behalf, all the conditions which were necessary and right.

He has borne the penalty of human weakness and transgression. He has met all demands for a perfect and unbroken obedience. He has engaged to secure, by the gift of the Holy Spirit, a holiness in us which could never have been obtained by our own efforts. And as He has become our Sponsor and Surety, so God is able to enter into these liberal terms with us, saying nothing of all the cost to His Son, but permitting us to share all the benefits, on this condition only, that we identify ourselves with Him by a living faith, entrusting all spiritual transactions into His hands, and abiding by the decisions of His will. This is the new and better covenant, which has replaced the old.

CHAPTER 20: THE HEAVENLY THINGS THEMSELVES

"For there was a tabernacle made." HEBREWS 9.2.

THE eye is quicker than the ear. And there is therefore no language so expressive as the language of symbols. The multitude will better catch your meaning by one apt symbol than by a thousand words. The mind shrinks from the intellectual effort of grappling with the subtle essences of things, and loves to have truth wrapped up in a form which can easily be taken in by the eye, the ear, the sense of touch.

This explains why there is such a tendency toward ritualism in the Romanish and Anglican Churches. Where man's spiritual life is strong, it is independent of the outward form, but when it is weak it leans feebly on external aids.

And it was because the children of Israel were in so childish a condition that God enshrined His deep and holy thoughts in outward forms and material shadows. The untutored people must have spiritual truth expressed in symbols, which appealed to the most obtuse. For fifteen hundred years, therefore, the Jewish worship gathered round the most splendid ceremonial that the world has ever seen, ceremonial which these Hebrew Christians sadly missed when they passed into the simple ordinances of some bare upper room.

Let us for a moment study those ancient symbols. Choose an expanse of sand. Mark out an oblong space forty-five feet long by fifteen feet broad. Lay all along upon your outlines a continuous belt of silver sockets, hollowed out so as to hold the ends of the planks that form the walls of the Tabernacle. Now fetch those boards themselves, beams of acacia wood fifteen feet high, covered with the choicest gold, and fastened together by three long bars of gold, running from end to end.

The entrance doorway must face the East, composed of five golden pillars, over which fall the folds of a rich and heavy curtain. Then measure thirty feet from this, and let another curtain separate the holy from the most Holy Place. Now fetch more curtains to make the ceiling, and to hang down on either side over the gilded acacia beams that form the outer walls. First, a gorgeous curtain wrought with brilliant hues, and covered with the forms of cherubim, next, a veil of pure white linen, third, a strong curtain of rams' skins, dyed red, and, lastly, to defend it from the weather, a common and coarse covering of badgers' skins. The court is constituted by heavy curtains that hang around and veil the movements of the priests within.

Let us cast a brief glance at each item as we briefly pass from the outer to the inner shrine.

THE BRAZEN ALTAR, with its projecting horns, to which animals designated for sacrifice were tied (Psalm 118.27), or on which the fugitive laid hold for sanctuary and shelter (Exodus 21.14), stood in the outer court. There were offered the sin offering, the burnt offering, and the peace offering. It was deemed most holy (Exodus 29.37). And well it might be, for it was the symbol of the cross of Calvary, that wondrous cross where Jesus offered Himself as a sacrifice for sin, Himself both priest and victim and altar too.

None could enter the holy place save by passing this sacred emblem, any more than we could ever have entered into fellowship with God, unless there had been wrought for us upon the cross that one all-sufficient sacrifice and oblation for sins, which purges our heart from an evil conscience. The longer we live, and the more we know of God, the more precious and indispensable does that cross appear. It is our hope in sorrow, our beacon in the dark, our shelter in the storm, our refuge in hours of conviction, our trysting-place with God, our pride and joy.

Blest cross! blest sepulchre! blest rather be
The Man that there was put to death for me."
And if the brazen altar speaks of the one sacrifice, once for all, of Calvary, the laver speaks of

the daily washing of the stains of our wilderness journeyings, as Jesus washed the feet of His disciples (John 13).

THE SEVEN-BRANCHED CANDLESTICK, from which the light was shed which lit up the holy place, would first arrest the eye of the priest, who might cross the threshold for the first time. Its form is familiar to us from the bas-relief on the Arch of Titus. How eloquently does it speak of Christ!

The texture of beaten gold, on every part of which the hammer strokes had fallen, tells of His bruisings for us (Exodus 25.36). The union of the six lesser lamps, with the one tall Centre one, betokens the mystery of that union in light-giving which makes the Church one with her Lord, for evermore in illuminating a dark world. The golden oil, stealing through the golden pipes that needed to be kept clean and unchoked, shows our dependence on Him for supplies of the daily grace of the Holy Spirit (Zechariah 4.2).

And the very snuffers, all of gold, used wisely by the high-priest to trim the flame, are significant of those processes by which our dear Lord is often obliged to cut away the unevenness of the wick, and to cause us a momentary dimming of light that we may afterward burn more clearly and steadily. His life is the light of men. In His light we see light. He sheds light on hearts and homes and mysteries and space, and hereafter the Lamb shall be the light of heaven.

THE GOLDEN SHEWBREAD TABLE must not be overlooked, with its array of twelve loaves of fine flour, sprinkled with sweet smelling frankincense, and eaten only by the priests, when replaced on the seventh day by a fresh supply. Here again, as in the last symbol, is that mysterious blending of Christ and His people.

Christ is the true bread of presence. He is the bread of God. Jehovah finds in His obedience and life and death perfect satisfaction. And we too feed on Him. His flesh is meat indeed. We eat His flesh and live by Him.

The table was portable, so as to be carried in the journeyings of the people, and we can never thrive without taking Him with us wherever we go. This is the heavenly manna, our daily bread; our priestly perquisite.

But the people also were represented in those twelve loaves, as they were in the twelve stones of the breastplate. And doubtless there is a sense in which all believers still stand ever before God in the purity and sweetness of Christ. "For we, being many, are one bread and one body, for we are all partakers of that one bread." Oh, is it possible for me to give aught of satisfaction to God? To believe this would surely instil a new meaning into the most trivial acts of life. Yet this may be so.

THE CENSER, OR ALTAR OF INCENSE, is classed with the Most Holy Place, not because it stood inside the veil, but because it was so closely associated with the worship rendered there. It was as near as possible to the ark (Exodus 30.6). It reminds us of the golden altar which was before the throne (Revelation 8.3).

No blood ever dimmed the lustre of the gold. The ashes that glowed there were brought from the altar of burnt offering, and on them was sprinkled the incense, which had been compounded by very special art (Exodus 30.34-38). That precious incense, which it was death to imitate, speaks of His much merit, in virtue of which our prayers and praises find acceptance. Is not this His perpetual work for us, standing in heaven as our great High Priest? Ever living to make intercession, catching our poor prayers, and presenting them to His Father, fragrant with the savour of His own grace and loveliness and merit?

THE VEIL, passed only once a year by the high-priest, carrying blood, reminded the worshippers that the way into the Holiest was not yet perfect. There were degrees of fellowship with God to which those rites could give no introduction. "The way into the holiest was not yet made manifest."

"The veil, that is to say, His flesh" (Hebrews 10.20). Oh, fine twined linen, in your purity, you were never so pure as that body which was conceived without sin! Oh, exquisite work of curious imagery, you cannot vie with the marvellous mysteries that gather in that human form! Yet, until Jesus died, there was a barrier, an obstacle, a veil. It was bespattered with blood, but it was a veil still.

But at the hour when He breathed out His soul in death, the veil was rent by mighty unseen hands from top to bottom, disclosing all the sacred mysteries beyond to the unaccustomed eyes of any priests who at that moment may have been burning incense at the hour of prayer, while the whole multitude stood outside.

The way into the Holiest lies open. It is new and living and blood-marked. We may therefore tread it without fear or mistake, and pass in with holy boldness to stand where angels veil their faces with their wings in ceaseless adoration (10.19, 20).

THE ARK. A box, oblong in shape, 4 ft. 6 in. in length, by 2 ft. 8 in. in breadth, its height; made of acacia wood, overlaid with gold, its lid, a golden slab, called the Mercy-seat, on which cherubic forms stood or knelt, with eyes fixed on the blood stained golden slab between them, for it was on the Mercy-seat that the blood was copiously sprinkled year by year, and there the Shekinah light ever shone.

In the wilderness wanderings the ark contained the tables of stone, not broken but whole, the manna, and the rod. But when it came to rest, and the staves were drawn out, the manna, food for pilgrims, and the rod, which symbolised the power of life, were gone. Only the law remained.

The law can never be done away with. It is holy, just, and good. Not one jot or tittle can pass away from it. It is at the heart of all things. Beneath all surfaces, below all coverlets, deeper than the foam and tumult and revolution of the world, rests righteous and inexorable law. We must all yield to its imperial sway. Even the atheist must build his walls according to the dictates of the plumb-line, or they will inevitably crumble to ruin.

But law is below love. The golden Mercy-seat exactly covered and hid the tablets, as they no longer leaped from crag to crag, but lay quietly beneath it. An ark without a covering, and from which tables of stony law looked out on one, would be terrible indeed. But there need be no dread to those who know that God will commune with them from above a Mercy-seat which completely meets the case and is sprinkled with blood.

We are told by the Apostle, who had well read the deepest meaning of these types, that "God has set forth Christ Jesus as a Mercy seat, through faith in his blood" (Romans 3.24, 25). Jesus has met the demands of law by His golden life and His death of blood, and we may meet God's righteousness in Him. Our own righteousness would be an insufficient covering, too narrow and too short, but our Substitute has met every possible demand. "Who is he that condemns ? It is Christ that died." Grace reigns through righteousness unto eternal life.

But ah, no blood of goat or calf can speak the priceless value of His blood, by which we have access into the Holiest. Oh, precious blood, which tells of a heart breaking with love and sorrow, which betrays a life poured out like water on the ground in extremest agony, which gathers up all the meaning of Leviticus and its many hecatombs of victims, the pledge of tenderest friendship, the purchase money of our redemption, the wine of life. Your scarlet thread speaks to us from the windows of the past in symbols of joy and hope and peace and immortal love. The precious blood of Christ!

CHAPTER 21: TEACHING BY CONTRAST

"How much more shall the blood of Christ, who through the Eternal Spirit offered Himself without spot to God, purge your conscience from dead works to serve the living God! (HEBREWS 9.14).

In this marvellous paragraph (verses 6-14) there are five striking and well-defined contrasts between the picture symbols of Leviticus, and the realities revealed in the New Testament Scriptures. And to their consideration we will at once proceed, thanking God as we do so that we live in the very midst of the heavenly things themselves, rather than in the shadows, which, though they doubtless helped and nourished the devout souls of an earlier age, were confessedly inadequate to supply the deeper demands of man's spiritual life.

THE FIRST TABERNACLE IS CONTRASTED WITH THE TRUE (verses 6, 8, 11). It must have been a fair and lovely sight to behold, when first, on the plains of Sinai, the Tabernacle was reared, with its golden furniture and sumptuous drapery. The very angels may have desired to look into it, and trace the outlines of thoughts, which perhaps were only beginning to unfold themselves to their intelligence.

But fair though it was, it had in it all those traces of imperfection which necessarily attach to human workmanship, and make even a needlepoint seem coarse beneath the microscope. It was "made with hands."

Besides which it was destined to grow old, and perish beneath the gnawing tooth or fret of time. Already it must have shown signs of decay when it was carefully borne across the Jordan, and, in David's days, its venerable associations could not blind him to the necessity of replacing it as soon as possible.

How different to this is the true tabernacle, of which it was the type, which is so much "greater and more perfect." What is that tabernacle? and where? Sometimes it seems to pious musing as if the whole universe were one great temple, the mountains its altars, the seas and oceans, with their vast depths, its lavers, the heavens its blue curtains, the loftier spaces, with their stars and mystery of colour, and fragrant incense-breath and angel worship, its holy place, whilst the very throne-room of God, where the Seer's eye beheld the rainbow-circled throne, corresponds to the Most Holy place in which the light of the Shekinah glistened over the bloodstained mercy seat.

But such poetic flights are forbidden by the sober prose which tells us that the true tabernacle is not "of this creation" (verse 11). It is no part of this created world, whether earth or heaven. It would exist, though all the material universe should resolve itself into primeval chaos. It is a spiritual fabric, whose aisles are trodden by saintly spirits in their loftiest experiences, when, forgetting that they are creatures of time, they rise into communion with God, and enjoy rapturous moments, which seem ages in their wealth of blessed meaning. Such is the true tabernacle which the Lord pitched, and not man (8.2).

THE HIGH-PRIESTS ARE CONTRASTED WITH CHRIST (verses 7,11). The outer court of the sanctuary might be trodden, under certain conditions, by ordinary Israelites, but for the most part they were excluded, and service was rendered by Levites and priests, at the head of whom stood the high-priest, radiant in his garments of glory and beauty.

The garment of fine white linen worn next his person, the linen girdle girt about his loins fitting him for ministry (John 13.4), the robe of the ephod, woven all of blue, and fringed with scarlet tassels in the form of pomegranates, the ephod itself, composed of the same materials as constituted the veil, and on his breast the twelve precious stones, engraved with the names of Israel. How grand a spectacle was there!

And yet there were two fatal flaws. He was not suffered to continue by reason of death (7.23); and he was a sinful man, who needed to offer sacrifice for himself (9.7). On the great day of atonement, it was expressly stated that he was not to go within the veil to plead for the people, until he had made an atonement for himself and his house by the blood of the young bullock, which he had previously killed (Leviticus 16.3, 6, 11-13).

In these respects, how different is our High-Priest, after the order of Melchizedek! Death tried to master Him, but He could not be held by it, and by death He destroyed him who has the power of death. "He continues ever." "He ever lives." His priesthood is unchangeable. "He is a priest forever." All this was clearly proved in the seventh chapter.

But now it is asserted that He was "without spot" (verse 14). He was well searched, but none could convince Him of sin. Judas tried to find some warrant for his treachery, but was compelled to confess that it was innocent blood. Caiaphas and Annas called in false witnesses in vain, and at last condemned Him on words uttered by His own lips, claiming divine authority and power. Pilate repeatedly asseverated, even washing his hands in proof, that he could find in Him no fault at all.

No, the Lord Himself bared His breast to the Father in conscious innocence, unlike the saintliest of men, who, in proportion to their goodness, confess their sinnership. "Such a High-Priest became us, who is holy, harmless, undefiled, and separate from sinners, who needs not daily to offer up sacrifice for His own sins.

THE VEILED WAY INTO THE HOLIEST IS CONTRASTED WITH OUR FREEDOM TO ENTER THE PRESENCE OF GOD. We have the positive assurance of these words that the Holy Spirit meant to signify direct spiritual truth in the construction of the Jewish Tabernacle (verse 8). He Who revealed divine truth by inspired prophets, revealed it so in the structure of the material edifice. The methods of instruction might vary, the teacher was the same. Indeed, the whole ritual was a parable for the present time (verse 9).

Every well-taught child is aware of the distinction between the holy place, with its candlesticks, incense-table, and shew-bread, and the Holy of Holies, with its ark, and cloud of glory. The first tabernacle was separated from the second by heavy curtains, which were never drawn aside except by the high-priest, and by him only once a year, and then in connection with an unusually solemn ritual.

Surely the dullest Israelite must have understood the meaning of that expressive figure, and have felt that, even though his race might claim to be nearer to God than all mankind beside, yet there was a depth of intimacy from which his foot was checked by the prohibition of God Himself. "The way into the holiest was not yet revealed."

For us, however, the veil is torn in two. Jesus entered once into the Holy place, and as he passed the heavy folds were rent in two from the top to the bottom. Surely no priest that witnessed it could ever forget the moment, when, as the earth trembled beneath the temple floor, the thickly woven veil split and fell back, and disclosed the solemnities on which no eyes but those of the high-priest dared to gaze.

Surely the most obtuse can read the meaning signified herein by the Holy Spirit. There is no veil between us and God but that which we weave by our own sin or ignorance. We may go into the very secrets of His love. We may stand unabashed where angels worship with veiled faces. We may behold mysteries hidden from before the foundation of the world. The love of God has no secrets for us whom He calls friends.

Oh, why are we so content with the superficial and the transient, with the ephemeral gossip and literature of our times, with the outer courts in which the formalists and worldly Christians around us are contented to remain, when there are such heights and depths, such lengths and breadths, to be explored in the very nature of God? Why do men in our time bring back that veil, though they call it "a screen"? Alas, they are blind leaders of the blind.

THE RITES OF JUDAISM ARE CONTRASTED WITH CONSCIENCE-CLEANSING ORDINANCES OF THE GOSPEL. They stood in meats and drinks and divers washings, which at the best were carnal ordinances imposed until a time of reformation, and though they rendered the worshiper ceremonially clean, they left his conscience unappeased.

A great many of the offences which required to be put away in those olden days arose from the breach of ceremonial laws. A man who touched the dead or the unclean became ceremonially defiled. For any such thing he must undergo the appointed rites of cleansing, ere he could enter the courts of the Lord's house.

The ceremonial laws were quite competent to deal with delinquencies like these, but they failed in providing atonement or in securing pardon for acts of sin. "They could not make him that did the service perfect, as pertaining to the conscience."

The unsatisfactory nature of sacrifices was even patent on the great day of atonement, which is here evidently referred to. Laying aside the gorgeous robes in which he was usually arrayed, the high-priest clothed himself in simple linen. The animals to be offered during the day were next presented at the door of the Tabernacle, and lots were cast as to which of the two bullocks was to be for himself, and which of the two goats was to be slain.

Then for the first time he entered the Most Holy place amid the fumes of fragrant incense, and sprinkled the blood of the bullock to make an atonement for the sins of himself and his house.

A second time he entered with the blood of the goat, to make an atonement for the sins of the people, who, meanwhile, stood without in penitential grief. And when all was over, the nation's sins were confessed over the head of the living goat, which was sent into the land of forgetfulness.

Still, no one could suppose that the slaying of the one goat or the sending of the other into the wilderness actually expiated the offence of the whole people. There was a remembrance of sins made once a year; but not necessarily entire remission for all who stood in that vast silent crowd. And many must have turned away in doubt and misgiving. David expressed their feeling when he sang the fifty-first Psalm beneath the impression of his own sinnership (see also Micah 6.6).

But how different is all this now! Our consciences are purged (verse 14). We have no more conscience of sins. We feel that the death of our Lord Jesus is an adequate expiation for them all, and that He has so fully taken them from us and put them away so that they cannot be found. They are as though they had never been. They have ceased from the very memory of God.

True, there are works which are constantly rendering our conscience unclean, as of old the flesh of the Israelite was rendered unclean by the touch of death. But the blood of Jesus does for our conscience what the ashes of the heifer did for the flesh of the ceremonially unclean. "The blood of Jesus Christ His Son cleanses us from all sin." We have therefore no longer an evil conscience resulting from unexpiated sin.

THE BLOOD OF ANIMALS IS CONTRASTED WITH THE BLOOD OF CHRIST.
Hecatombs of victims are not of equal value with one man. How much less with the Son of God! Rivers of the blood of beasts are not equivalent to one drop of His. They offer no standard by which to apprise His precious blood. This is too obvious to need further comment here, and we shall need to defer to another chapter our estimate, however inadequate, of the value of that blood.

But in the meanwhile, let us notice that it was through the Eternal Spirit that Christ offered Himself without spot to God. It was not, as some falsely affirm, that the Father forced an innocent man to suffer for sins he had never done, or that our Saviour suffered to appease the Father's wrath, but that the eternal nature of God came out in the sacrifice of Calvary. "God was in Christ, reconciling the world unto Himself."

When God determined to save men, He did not delegate the work to angels, nor did He permit a sinless man to sink beneath the intolerable burden of a world's sin, but in the person of His Son, He took home to Himself the agony and curse and cost of sin, and by bearing them, wiped them out forever. It is, therefore, eternal redemption (verse 12).

The death of the cross was a voluntary act. "He offered Himself. " He was priest and victim both. And it was an act in which the Eternal Trinity participated, the manifestation in time of an eternal fact of the divine nature.

And how can we ever show our gratitude, except by serving the living God (verse 14). We are redeemed to serve, bought to be owned absolutely. Who can refuse a service so reasonable, fraught with blessedness so transcendent? Head! think for Him whose brow was thorn-girt. Hands! toil for Him whose hands were nailed to the cross. Feet! speed to do His behests whose feet were pierced. Body of mine! be His temple whose body was wrung with pains unspeakable. To serve Him - this is the Only true attitude and behaviour, as those who are not their own, but His.

CHAPTER 22: THE BLOOD OF CHRIST

"Without shedding of blood is no remission." -HEBREWS 9.22.

Round and round this ancient window into the past (verses 15-28) is bound the red cord of blood. Twelve times at the very least does this solemn, this awful, word occur. The Devil himself seems to admit that it is invested with some mystic potency; else why should he compel so many of his miserable followers to interlard each phrase they utter by some reference to it?

Man cannot look on or speak of blood without an involuntary solemnity, unless, indeed, he has done despite to some of the deepest instincts of his being, or through familiarity has learned contempt. And we feel whilst reading this chapter, as if we have come into the very heart of the deepest of all mysteries, the most solemn of all solemnities, the most awful of all tragedies or martyrdoms or sacrificial rites. Take off the shoes from your feet, for the place on which we stand together now is holy ground.

Blood is becoming increasingly recognised as one of the most important constituents of the human body. Scientific and other research is more and more inclined to verify the ancient sayings, which may have been broken in the colleges of Egypt, where Moses learned the most advanced science of his time, before ever they were stamped with the imprimatur of inspiration. "the blood is the life", "the life of the flesh is in the blood" (Deuteronomy 12.23; Leviticus 17.2).

We know that the red corpuscles of the blood play an important function in carrying the oxygen of the air to consume the decaying tissues, and to light fires in every part of the human frame. But who can tell all the mysterious functions of the numberless colourless disks which float along the currents of the blood, and which may be intimately connected with the very essence of our vitality? Certain it is that impoverished blood means decrepit life, tainted blood means corruption and disease, ebbing blood means waning life.

The first effort of the physician is to feel the pulse of the blood, whilst the most fatal disease is the poisoning of the blood. The blood is the life. And shed blood is life poured forth from its source and fountainhead.

There is nothing, therefore, in man more precious than blood. If he gives that, he gives the best he has to give. His blood is his life - his all, and it is a noble act when a man is ready to make this supreme gift for others. It is this which lights up the devilry of war, and sheds a transient gleam of nobility on the coarsest, roughest soldiery, that they are prepared to sacrifice their lives in torrents of blood, to beat the foeman back from hearth and home and fatherland.

This is why women have treasured up handkerchiefs dipped in the blood that has flowed on the headsman's block from the veins of martyrs for liberty or religion. This is why men point without a shudder to the stains of blood on blades that have been drawn in freedom's holy cause, or on tattered banners which led the fight against the battalions of Paganism or Popery.

This is why the historian of the Church does not feel too dainty to make frequent reference to the blood which flowed in rivers on the eve of the Sicilian Vespers, and on the day of black St. Bartholomew.

No, we glory in the blood which noble men have poured out as water on the ground. None of us is too sensitive to dwell with exultation on the phrase.

Why, then, should we hesitate to speak of the blood of Christ? It was royal blood. "His own" (verse. 12), and He was a King indeed. It was voluntarily shed. " He offered Himself" (verse 14). It was pure "innocent blood," "without spot" (verse 14). It was sacrificial. He died not as a martyr, but as a Saviour (verse 26).

It flowed from His head, thorn-girt, that it might atone for sins of thought, from His hands and feet, fast nailed, that it might expiate sins of deed and walk, from His side, that it might wipe out the sins of our affections, as well as tell us of His deep and fervent love, which could not be confined within the four chambers of His heart, but must find vent in falling on the earth.

Why should we be ashamed of the blood of Christ? No other phrase will so readily or sufficiently gather up all the complex thoughts which mingle in the death of Christ. Life. Life shed. Life shed violently. Life shed violently, and as a sacrifice. Life passing forth by violence, and sacrificially, to become a tide of which we must also all stoop down and drink, if we desire to have life in ourselves (John 6.53-56).

"This is He that came by water and blood. Not by water only, but by water and blood" (1 John

5.6). Oh, precious words, recalling that never-to-be-forgotten incident when, following the rugged point of the soldier's spear, there came out blood and water from the Saviour's broken heart (John 19.34).

Had it been water only, we had been undone. Water might do for respectable sinners, fifty pence debtors, Pharisees, who are not sinners as other men. But some of us feel water would be of no avail at all. Our sins are so deep-dyed, so inveterate, so fast, that nothing but blood could set us free. Blood must atone for us. Blood must cleanse us. In other words, life must be shed to redeem us, such life as is poured from the very being of the Son of God.

But there is a deep sense in which that blood is flowing, washing, cleansing, and feeding soul, all down the age. Like the stream of desert, it follows us. "It speaks" pleading with God for man, and with man for God (12.24). "It cleanses," not as a single past act, but as a perpetual experience in the believer's soul, removing recent sin, and checking the uprisings of our evil nature (1 John 1.7). It is the drink of all devout souls, and its perennial presence and efficacy is well symbolised by the appearance still on the communion table of the church of the wine, which tells the worshipper that the blood of Calvary, once shed, and never shed again, is as fresh and efficacious as ever, or as the wine poured freshly into the cup.

Let men say what they will, the shedding of the blood of Christ is an embodiment of an eternal fact in the Being of God, and is an essential condition of the healthy life of man.

It purges the defiled conscience more completely than the ashes of a heifer purged of flesh of the ceremonially unclean (verse 14). Why, then, do you carry about the perpetual consciousness of sin? Confess sin instantly, whenever you are aware of it. Claim the blood of sprinkling, and go at once to serve the living God.

It put away the sin of previous dispensation. It was in virtue of the death to be suffered on Calvary that the holy God was able to forgive the offences and accept the imperfect services of Old Testament saints. The shadow of the cross fell backward, as well as forward. And it is because of what Jesus did that all have been saved, who have passed within the pearly gate, or shall pass it (verse 15, and compare Romans 3.25; 4.24).

It ratifies the covenant. No covenant was ratified in the old time, except in blood. When God entered into covenant with Abraham, five victims were divided in the midst, making a lane, down which the fire-symbol of the divine presence passed. "There is of necessity the death of the covenant maker." And in pursuance of this ancient custom, the first covenant was solemnly sealed by blood (verses 18,19). How sure and steadfast must that covenant be into which God has entered with our Surety on our behalf! The blood of Jesus is an asseveration which cannot be gainsaid or transgressed. All God's will is opened to us since Jesus died. We may claim what we will. We are His heirs, the heirs of the wealth of our Elder Brother, Jesus.

It opens the way into the Holiest. What the high-priest did every year in miniature, Christ has done once (verses 24, 25, 26). "He died unto sin once." By virtue of His own shed blood, He went once for all into the real Holiest place, appearing in the presence of God for us as our High-Priest, and leaving the way forever open to those who dare to follow.

"The heavenly things themselves" need cleansing, not because of any intrinsic evil in themselves, but because they are constantly being used and trodden by sinful men. Now, however, though that is so, there is an efficacy in the work of Jesus which is always counterveiling our impurity, and making it possible for us to draw near to God with boldness and acceptance.

It put away sin "once for all." "Once in the end of the world." Not for each dispensation, but for all dispensations. Not for one age, but for all ages Not for a few, but for the "many," comprehending the vastness of the number which no man can compute of the great family of man. As the year's sin of a nation was borne away into the desert by the scapegoat, and put away, so was the whole sin of the race centred on the head of Jesus. He was made sin. As a physician might be imagined drawing on himself all the maladies of his patients, so did Jesus draw to Himself and assume all the sins of mankind. He was the propitiation for the whole world.

And when He died, He dropped sin as a stone into the depths of oblivion. And He put away sin. The Greek word is very strong, 'annihilated, made nothing of, made as though it had never been'. Sin, in the mind and purpose of God, is as entirely done away as a debt when it is paid. Hallelujah! in heaven and on earth (Revelation 5.9; 1.5).

But whilst this is an eternal truth with Him who knows not our distinctions of time, yet it will avail only as a fact when each individual sinner lays claim to this wonderful provision, confesses his sin, and realises that there is now no longer condemnation, because the Lamb of God has borne away His sin and the world's. Will you now dare to reckon this to be true for you, not because you feel it, but because God says it? Dare to repeat 1 Peter 2.24, and Isaiah 53.5, substituting "my" for "our.

"What marvellous appearances are these three! He appeared once in the end of the world as a sacrifice. He appears now in heaven as a Priest. He will appear the second time without sin unto salvation, as of old the high priest, at the close of the day of atonement, came out with outstretched hands to bless the people. Oh, to be looking for Him, that we may not miss the radiant vision or the tender blessing of peace!

CHAPTER 23: "ONCE"

"Once in the end of the world has He appeared, to put away sin by the sacrifice of Himself." (HEBREWS 9.26).

THERE is a word here which recurs, like a note on an organ beneath the tumult of majestic sound. Five times, at least, it rolls forth its thunder, pealing through all ages, echoing through all worlds, announcing the finality of an accomplished redemption to the whole universe of God "ONCE!"

And there is another phrase which we must couple with it, spoken by the parched lips of the dying Saviour, yet with a loud voice, as though it were the cry of a conqueror: "When Jesus, therefore, had received the vinegar, He said, 'It is finished'; and He bowed His head and gave up the ghost."

It is very seldom that man can look back on a finished life-work. The chisel drops from the paralysed hand ere the statue is complete, the chilling fingers refuse to guide the pen along another line, though the book is so nearly done, the statesman must leave his plans and far-reaching schemes to be completed by another, perhaps his rival. But as from His cross Jesus Christ our Lord looked upon the work of redemption which He had undertaken, and in connection with which He had suffered even to the hiding of his Father's face, He could not discover one stitch, or stone, or particle deficient.

For untold myriads, for you and me and all, there was done that which never needed to be done again, but stood as an accomplished fact forevermore.

THE "ONCE" OF A COMPLETED WORK (9.26). In these words there is a sigh of relief. A thought had for a moment flashed across the sunlit page of Scripture, which had suggested an infinite horror. In pursuing the parallels between the incidents of the great day of atonement and the great day when Jesus died, we had been suddenly reminded of the fact that the solemn spectacle was witnessed once a year "

The high-priest enters into the Holy place every year with blood of others" (verse 25). Every year the same rites performed, the same blood shed, the same propitiation made. Suppose that, after the same analogy, Jesus had suffered every year! Every year the agony of the shadowed garden! Every year the bitter anguish of the cross! Every year the burial in the garden tomb! Then earth would have been overcast with midnight, and life would have been agony! Who could bear to see Him suffer often!

But there was no necessity for Him to suffer more than once, because repetition means imperfection, of which, in His work, there is no sign or trace. The repetition of the sacrifices of the Jewish law meant that they could not take away sin, or make the comers thereunto perfect. Again and again the crowd of pious Jews gathered, driven to seek deliverance from the conscience of sins, which brooded deeply and darkly over their souls.

Perhaps they would receive momentary respite as they saw the elaborate ceremonial, and felt that they were included in the high-priest's confession and benediction. And so they wended their way homeward, but ere long a weary sense of dissatisfaction would again betake them. They would reflect on the inadequacy of the atonement which stood only in the offering of the life of slain beasts.

Sins were remembered, but not put away. It was impossible that the blood of bulls and goats could do that (10.4). And so, doubtless, in the more thoughtful, hearts must have failed, and consciences moaned out their weary plaint unsatisfied. Therefore the sacrifices had to be presented continually.

On the other hand, Christ's work needs no repetition. It is final because it is perfect. Its perfection is attested, because it has never been repeated. "In that He died, He died to sin once." Our Saviour set His hand to save us. He did not mean to fail. He came into our world with this distinct purpose. He died to do it. And, having done it, He went home to God. But if from the vantage-ground of the throne, reviewing His work, He had discerned any deficiency or flaw, He would have come back to make it good, and, inasmuch as He has not done so, we may be sure that the death of the cross is perfectly satisfactory.

"Now once, in the end of the ages, has He appeared to put away sin by the sacrifice of Himself." Oh, ponder these wondrous words! Once. He lives forevermore, and will never again pass for a moment under the dark shadow of death.

He has appeared (or been manifested). What then? He must have existed previously. The incarnation was but the embodiment in visible form of One who existed before all worlds, and the death of the cross was the unfolding in a single act of eternal facts in the nature of God. As the great sun-disk may be mirrored in a tiny mountain lake, so in the one day of crucifixion, there were set forth to men, angels, and devils, love, sacrifice, and redeeming mercy, which are part of the very essence of God. Marvellous, indeed, the rending of the veil, by which such marvels are revealed.

In the end of the world (or of the ages). God is called the King of Ages. Time is probably as much a creation as space or distance or matter. It is an accommodation to finite thought, a parenthesis in eternity, a rainbow flung across the mighty age of deity.

We break time into hours, God breaks it into ages. There are ages behind us, and ages before. We stand on a narrow neck of land between two seas.

The first age of which we know anything is that of creation. The second, of Paradise. The third, of the world before the flood. The fourth, of the Patriarchs. The fifth, of Moses, ending with the fall of Jerusalem, and the death of the Messiah. The sixth, of the Gentiles, in which we live. And before us, we can dimly descry the forms of the Age of Regeneration and Restitution, the Age of Judgment, and the Age in which the kingdom shall be delivered to the Father. There is thus a complete analogy between the creation of the material world, and the creation of the new heavens and earth.

Geologists love to enumerate the strata of the earth's formation through which the processes of world -building were carried, and we will probably discover some day that God has been building up the new creation through successive ages of history and development. Christ's death is here said to have happened at the end of the ages, and we should at once see the force of this, even though there may remain several great ages to be fulfilled, ere time run out its course, if only we knew how many ages have preceded.

Compared to the number that have been, this is the end, the climax, the ridge of the weary climb. What lies beyond are the miles of level surface, to the sudden dip down of the cliffs in face of the ocean of eternity.

He has put away sin. Oh, marvellous word! It might be rendered to annihilate, to make as if it had never been. The wreath of cloud may disappear, but the separated drops still float through space. The bubble may break on the foam-tipped wave, but the film of water has gone to add its attenuated addition to the ocean depth. But Jesus has put sin away as when a debt is paid, an obligation is cancelled, or a sin-laden victim was slain, burned, and buried in the old days of Moses.

All sin, the sin of the world, the accumulated sin of mankind was made to meet in Jesus. He was made sin. He stood before the universe as though He had drawn upon Himself all the human sin which has ever rent the air or befouled the earth, or put the stars of night to the blush, and, bearing the shame, the horror, the penalty during those dread hours which rung from Him the cry of desolate forsakenness, He put it away, and wiped it out forever, and, in doing this, He has put away the penal results of Adam's fall.

The inherited tendencies to evil remain in all the race, but the spiritual penalty which Adam incurred for himself and all of us, as our representative and head, has been cancelled by the sufferings and death of our glorious representative and head, the Second Adam, the Lord from heaven.

Men will still have to suffer the penalty of sins which they voluntarily commit, and for which they do not seek forgiveness and cleansing through the blood, but men will not have to suffer the penalty which otherwise must have accrued to them, as members of a fallen race - fallen with their first parents and father, because Jesus put away that when He died.

And thus it is our hope that the multitudes of sweet babes, idiots, and others who belong to Adam's race, but have had no opportunity of personal transgression, are able to enter without let or hindrance into the land where there enters nothing which defiles.

By the sacrifice of Himself. Not by His example, fair and lovely though it was. Not by His teaching, though it was the food of the world. Not by His works, the source and fountain-head of modern philanthropy. But by His death, and by His death as a sacrifice.

If you want to understand a writer, you must know the sense in which he uses his characteristic words, and you must carefully study the definitions which he gives of them. And if you would understand the meaning of Christ's death, you must go back to the definitions, given in minute detail in Leviticus, of the meaning of sacrifice, atonement, and propitiation, by which that death is afterward described, and only so much you dare to interpret. Whatever sacrifice meant in Leviticus, it means when applied to the death of the cross. And surely there can be no controversy that of old it stood for the substitution of the innocent for the guilty, the cancelling of deserved penalty because it had been borne by another, the wiping out of sin by the shedding of blood.

All this it must mean when applied to the death of Christ, with this difference, that of old the suffering was borne and death endured involuntarily, but in the case of our blessed Redeemer, God in Him took home to Himself, voluntarily and freely, the accumulated results of a world's sin, and suffered them, and made them as if they had never been. "He put away sin by the sacrifice of himself."

What was the death of Christ? "A martyrdom," cries modern thought. "A mischance in an unenlightened age," replies the reviewer. "An outcome of all such efforts to battle with evil," says the broad-church teacher.

"A SACRIFICE!" thunders this Book. A voluntary sacrifice! A voluntary sacrifice by which sin has been borne and put away. Here we rest, content to abide, in a world of mystery, at the foot of one mystery more, which, despite all its mystery, answers the cry of a convicted conscience, and sheds the peace of heaven through our hearts.

THE "ONCE" OF MORTALITY (9.27). With a few exceptions mentioned on the page of Scripture, where miracles of raising are recounted, men die but once. For those there was one cradle, two coffins; one birth, two burials. But for most it is mercifully arranged that the agony and pain of dissolution should be experienced only once. And this, which is the ordinary lot of humanity, also befell Jesus Christ.

He could not die often, because he was literally man, and it would have been inconsistent to violate in His case the universal law. He must become man, because only through the portal of birth could He reach the river of death, but, having been born, and assumed our nature, He must obey the laws of that nature, and die but once.

THE "ONCE" OF DEITY (9.28). There must have been something more than mortal in Him, Who in His one death could bear away the sins of many. Good and great men have died, who would have done anything to cancel or atone for the sins of their nation, their family, and their beloved, but in vain. How marvellous then must be His worth, whose sufferings and death will counterveil for a world's sin!

And we can see the imperious necessity that our Saviour should be God manifest in the flesh, and that He Who became obedient to the death of the cross should be also He who was in the form of God, and thought it not robbery to be God's equal.

If it be true that His death "once" has put away sin, then, bring hither your songs of worship, your wreaths of empire, your ascriptions of lowliest adoration, for He must be God. No being of inferior make could do for man what, in that brief but dreadful darkness, He has done once for all, and forever.

THE "ONCE" OF A PURGED CONSCIENCE (10.2). We are not in the position of the Jews, needing to repeat their sacrifices year by year, in sad monotony; our sacrifice has been offered once for all. Therefore, we have not, like them, the perpetual conscience of sins. Our hearts are, once and forever, sprinkled from an evil conscience (verse 22).

There is no necessity to ask repeatedly for forgiveness for the sins that have been once confessed and forgiven. God does not accuse us of them, we need not accuse ourselves. God does not remember them, we may well forget them, save as incentives to gratitude and humility. There is daily need for fresh confession of recent sin, but when once the soul realises the completeness of Christ's work on its behalf, it cries with great joy: "As far as the east is from the west, so far has He removed our transgressions from us."

THE "ONCE" OF A FULFILLED PURPOSE (10.10). Space forbids our lingering longer. In our next chapter we may show how completely the purpose of God has been realised in Jesus, and, therefore, that there is no necessity for a repetition of His sacrificial work. The will or purpose of God for man's redemption asks for nothing more than that which is given it in the life and death of our Saviour. Nothing more is required for the glory of God, for the accomplishment of the divine counsels, or for the perfect deliverance and sanctification of those who believe.

CHAPTER 24: AN ANCIENT HEBREW CUSTOM

"Sacrifice and offering you desire not, but a body you have prepared me." (HEBREWS 10.5).

In that old Hebrew world that lies now so far back in the dim twilight of the past, there were several customs, of more than transient interest, one of which claims our thought as it glistens for a moment beneath the touch of this Epistle, as a wave far out to sea, when smitten for a moment by the sunlight.

It appears that if an Israelite, through the stress of bad seasons and disappointing harvests, were to fall into deep arrears to some rich neighbouring creditor - so much so that he owed him even more than the land of his inheritance was worth - he was permitted not only to alienate his land till the year of jubilee, but to sell his own service so as to work out his debt.

It must have been a very painful thing for the peasant proprietor to say farewell to his humble home and endeared possessions, in which his forefathers had lived and thrived, and to go forth into the service of another. Very affecting must have been the farewell walk around the tiny plot, which he and his might not live to revisit.

And yet the bitterness of the separation must have been greatly mitigated and lessened by the instant freedom from anxiety which ensued. No more dark forebodings for the future, no eager questioning of how to keep the wolf from the door, no unequal struggle with the adverse seasons. All responsibility - for the payment of other creditors, for supplies of food and clothing for himself and his wife and children - from henceforth must rest on the shoulders of another.

So the appointed six years passed away, and at their close the master would call the labourer into his presence, to give him his discharge. But at that moment he might, if he chose, bind himself to that master's service forever. If he shrank from facing the storms of poverty and difficulty, if he preferred the shelter and plenty of his master's home to the struggle for existence from which he had been so happily shielded, if, above all, he loved his master, and desired not to be separated from him again, he was at liberty to say so." I love my master, I will not go out free."

Then, solemnly, and before the judges, so that the choice was deliberately ratified, his master bored his ear through with an awl to the doorpost, leaving a permanent and indelible impression of the relationship into which they had entered. "And he shall serve him forever" (Exodus 21.6).

This custom was ALLUDED TO BY THE PSALMIST (Psalm 40.6). Living amid the routine of daily, monthly, and yearly sacrifices, this saint felt deeply their inability to take away sin, and saw that the true offering to God must be of another kind. What could he do adequately to express his sense of the wonderful works and countless thoughts of God! Surely the offered sacrifice of flour or blood, the burnt-offering or sin offering could not be the highest expression of human love and devotion.

And then he bethought him of a more excellent way. He will come to God, bearing in his hand the volume of the book of his will. His heart will dote on that holy transcript of his Father's character. Yes, he will translate its precepts into prompt and loving obedience. "I delight to do your will, 0h my God. Yes, your law is within my heart." " This will please the Lord better than an ox or bullock that has horns and hoofs."

Nor is this all. Recalling the ancient usage to which we have alluded, he imagines himself repeating the vow of the Hebrew bondservant, and standing meekly and voluntarily at God's door, while his ear is bored to it forever. Henceforth he may almost cry with the Apostle, "From henceforth let no man trouble me, for I bear branded on my body the marks of Jesus." "Mine ears you have bored." "Truly I am your servant, you have loosed my bonds."

We need not wonder at the glad outburst which succeeds (verse 10). As with emphatic and repeated phrase the Psalmist avows his intention of telling the great congregation his discoveries of the love of God, we can well understand the reason of his exultation.

There is no life so free as that which has escaped all other masters in becoming the bond-slave of Jesus. There is no nature so exuberant with joy and peace unspeakable as that which has felt the stab of the awl, has been tinged with the blood of self-sacrifice for His dear sake, and has passed through the open doorway to go out nevermore. There is no rest so unutterable as that which knows no further care, since all care has been once and forever laid on Him who can alone bear the pressure of sorrow and sin, responsibility and need.

APPROPRIATED BY THE LORD JESUS. In His incarnation our blessed Lord has realised all the noblest aspirations and assertions which had ever been spoken by the lips of His most illustrious saints. The very words used by them can, therefore, be literally appropriated by Him, without exaggeration, save where they falter with the broken confessions of sin and mortal weakness.

Amongst others, when he came into the world, He could take up those olden words of the Fortieth Psalm, and, through them, fulfil the meaning of the ancient Hebrew custom.

The sacrifices of Leviticus had served a very necessary purpose in familiarising men with the thoughts of God as to the true aspect in which our Saviour's death was to be viewed, but it was evident that they could not exhaust this idea, or fill up the measure of His redeeming purpose. His will went far beyond them all, and, therefore, they could not be other than incomplete, and, on account of their very incompleteness, they needed incessant repetition, and even then, though repeated for centuries, they could not accomplish the purposes on which the divine nature was set. As well fill up the ocean with cartloads of soil, as accomplish the measure of God's will by the blood of bulls and goats.

But when Jesus came into the world He at once set Himself to accomplish that holy will. This was His constant cry: "Lo, I come to do you will, 0 God! "And He not only essayed to do God's will in every minute particular and detail of His life, but especially where it touched the removal of sin, the redemption of men, the sanctification and perfecting of those who believe.

It was to accomplish God's will in these respects that the Saviour died on the cross. And it is because He perfectly succeeded, cutting out the entire pattern of the divine mind in the cloth of His obedience, that the ineffective sacrifices of Judaism have been put an end to, whilst His own sacrifice has not required the addition of a single sigh or tear or hour of darkness or thrill of agony.

By the offering of His body once for all we have been sanctified, i.e. our judicial standing before God is completely satisfactory. And by one offering He has perfected forever them that are being sanctified, i.e. He has accomplished all the objective work of our redemption in such a way that in Him we stand before God as accepted saints, though much more has yet to be done in our subjective inward experience (Hebrews 10.10, 14).

The entire submission of our Lord to His Father's will comes out very sweetly in a slight change here made in quoting the ancient Psalm. It may be that some older version, or various reading, is given, with the sanction of the divine Spirit. Instead of saying "Mine ear you have opened," the Lord is represented as saying, "A body you have prepared for Me."

In point of fact, though the ear carried the body with it, because it is notoriously difficult to move hand or foot so long as the ear is a captive, yet the Hebrew slave only gave his ear to the piercing awl in token of his surrender. But our Lord Jesus gave, not His ear only, but His whole body, in every faculty and power. He held nothing back, but yielded to God the Father the entirety of that body which was prepared for Him by the Holy Spirit in the mystery of the holy incarnation.

Ah! blessed is our lot, that God's holy redemptive purpose has been so utterly and so efficiently fulfilled, through the offering of that body once for all nailed, not to the doorpost, but to the cross.

APPLICABLE TO OURSELVES. There is a strong demand among God's people in the present day for that "more abundant life" which the Good Shepherd came to bestow. Out of this demand is springing a mighty movement, which if it obey the following rules and conditions, will surely be a blessing to the Church.

It must be natural The saintliness that cannot romp and laugh with little children, and looks askance on the great movements in the world around, and shuts itself up in cloistered seclusion, is not the ideal of Jesus Christ, who watched the children playing in the market places, and called them to His arms, and mingled freely at the dinner-tables of the rich. It is easier, perhaps, than His, but it is a profound mistake to suppose that it will satisfy His heart. No. The saintliness of the true saint must find its home in the ordinary homes and haunts of men.

It must be humble. Directly a man begins to boast of what he has attained, you may be sure that he makes up in talk for what he lacks in vital experience. The tone with which some speak of perfection indicates how far they are from it. To brag of sinlessness is to yield to pride, the worst of sins. No face truly shines so long as its owner wists it. No heart is childlike which is conscious of itself.

It must lay stress on the objective side of Christ's work. There must be introspection for the detection and removal of anything that lies between the soul and God, just as there must be sometimes a discharge of gunpowder to dislodge the accumulated soot of a foul chimney. But when the necessary work of introspection and confession is over, there should be an instant return to God, with the devout outlook of the soul on the person and work of the Lord Jesus. We must never encourage the introspection, except with the view of a more uninterrupted vision of Jesus.

If these three conditions are complied with, the movement now afoot cannot but be fraught with blessing to the universal Church; and it will probably have the effect of leading multitudes to pass through an experience like that indicated in the Psalm. Previously they may have acted merely from a sense of legalism and duty, giving sacrifices and offerings as appointed by the law. But from the glad hour that they realise all the claims of Jesus on their emancipated and surrendered natures, they will exclaim, "We love our Master; we will not go out free. Bore our ears to His door, that we may serve Him forever. We delight to do His will. His law is within our hearts. We are eager to do all things written in the roll of the book of His will."

Have you ever uttered words like these? Has your life been only a monotonous round of unavoidable service, of which the key-word has been "must"? Alas! you have not as yet tasted how easy is His yoke, how light His burden. But if only from this moment you would open your whole heart to the work of the Holy Spirit, yielding fully to Him, He would shed the love of God abroad within you, kindling your love to Him, and, at once, you would do from love what you have done from law. You would be so knit to Christ that you would not be free from Him, even though you could do without Him. You would have forever the scar of the slavery of Jesus wrought into your very nature.

There is nothing in the world that gives so much rest to the soul as to do the will of God, whether it speaks on the page of Scripture, or through the inspirations of the Holy Spirit within the shrine of the heart, or in the daily routine of ordinary or extraordinary Providence.

If only we could always say, "I delight to do your will. I come, I come!" If only we could offer up to God, as Jesus did, the bodies which He has prepared for us, though to the very bitterness of the cross. If only we were as intent on finishing the work given us to do by Him, as men are in achieving the ends of personal ambition. Then the spirit of heaven, where the will of God is done, would engird our barren, weary lives, as the Gulf Stream some wintry shore, dispelling the frost and mantling the soil with flowers of fairest texture and fruits of Paradise.

Do not try to feel the will of God. Will it, choose it, obey it. And as time goes on, what you commenced by choosing you will end by loving with ardent and even vehement affection.

CHAPTER 25: DRAWING BACK

"The just shall live by faith, but if any man draw back, My soul shall have no pleasure in him." (HEBREWS 10.38).

The Epistle has been for some time glowing with ever-increasing heat, and now it flames out into a vehement expostulation, which must have startled and terrified those Hebrew Christians who were still wavering between Judaism and Christianity.

As we have had more than one occasion to remark, it had become a great question with some of them whether they should go back to the one, or go on with the other. The splendid ceremonial, venerable age, and old associations of Judaism, were fighting hard to wean them away from the simplicity and spiritual demands of the later faith. But surely the retrograde movement would be arrested, and the impetus toward Christ accelerated, by these sublime and soul-stirring remonstrances.

THE THREEFOLD CONCLUSION ALREADY ARRIVED AT is summed up in three momentous propositions.

We may boldly enter the Holiest by the blood of Jesus. The Holiest was the chamber of innermost communion with God. To enter it was to speak with God face to face. And its equivalent for us is the right to make our God our confidant and friend, into Whose secret ear we may pour the whole story of sin and sorrow and need.

Nor need the memory of recent sin distress us, because the blood of Jesus is the pledge of the forgiveness and acceptance of those who are penitent and believing. We may go continually, and even dwell, where Israel's high priests might tread but once each year.

Jesus has inaugurated a new and living way. The veil of the Temple was torn in two when Jesus died, to indicate that the way to God was henceforth free to man, without let or hindrance, and without the intervention of a human priest. Priests have tried to block it, and to compel men to pay them toll for opening it. But their pretensions are false. They have no such power. The way stands open still for every trembling seeker.

It is new, because, though myriads have trodden it, it is as fresh as ever for each new priestly foot. It is living, because it is through the living Saviour that we come to God. "No man comes to the Father but by me."

Stay here to note that the veil, with its curious workmanship, was a symbol of the body of Christ. "The veil, that is to say, His flesh." We get near to God through the death of that Son of man Who, in real human sorrow, hung on the cross for us.

We have a Great priest. We belong to the household of God by faith, but we need a Priest. Priests need a Priest. And such a one we have, who ever lives to make intercession for us, and to offer our prayers on the golden altar, mingled with the much incense of His own precious merit. These are the three conclusions which recapitulate the positions laid down and proved up to this point.

THE THREEFOLD EXHORTATION FOUNDED ON THE PREVIOUS CONCLUSIONS, "Let us draw near" (verse 22). "Let us hold fast" (verse 23). "Let us consider one another" (verse 24). And each of these three exhortations revolves around one of the three words which are so often found in combination in the Epistles - Faith, Hope, and Love (R.V).

FAITH consists of two parts - belief, which accepts certain declarations as true, and trust in the person about whom these declarations are made. Neither will do without the other. On the one hand, we cannot trust a person without knowing something about him, on the other hand, our knowledge will not help us unless it leads to trust, any more than it avails the shivering wretch outside the Bank of England to know that the vaults are stored with gold.

A mere intellectual faith is not enough. The holding of a creed will not save. We must pass from a belief in words to trust in the Word. By faith we know that Jesus lives, and by faith we also appropriate that life. By faith we know that Jesus made on the cross a propitiation for sin; and by faith we lay our hand reverently on His dear head and confess our sin.

Faith is the open hand receiving Christ. Faith is the golden pipe through which His fullness comes to us. Faith is the narrow channel by which the life that pulses in the Redeemer's heart enters our souls. Faith is the attitude we assume when we turn aside from the human to the divine.

We ought not to be content with anything less than the full assurance of faith. The prime method of increasing it is in drawing near to God. In olden days the bodies of the priests were bathed in water and sprinkled with blood ere they entered the presence of God. Let us seek the spiritual counterpart of this. Relieved from the pressure of conscious guilt, with hearts as sincere and guileless as the flesh is clean when washed with pure water, let us draw near to God and kneel in fellowship with him. And in that attitude faith will grow exceedingly. It will no longer sit in the dust, but clothe itself in beautiful garments. It will wax from a thread to become a cable. No longer the trembling touch of a woman's hand, it will grasp the pillars of the Temple with a Samson's embrace.

HOPE is more than faith, and has special reference to the unknown future which it realises, and brings to bear on our daily life. The veil that hides the future parts only as smitten by the prow of our advancing boat. It is natural, therefore, that we should often ask what lies beyond.

Foreboding is the prophet of ill, hope of good. Forebodingcries, "We shall certainly fall by the hand of ---, hope replies, "No weapon that is formed against us will prosper." Foreboding cries, "Who will roll away the stone? " Hope sings merrily, "The Lord will go before us, and make the crooked places straight." Foreboding, born of unbelief, cries, "The people are great and tall, and the cities walled up to heaven". Hope already portions out the land and chooses its inheritance.

But Christian hope is infinitely better and more reliable than that of the worldling. In ordinary hope there is always the element of uncertainty. It may be doomed to disillusionment and disappointment. Things may not turn out as we expect, and so, being the characteristic of youth, it dies down as the years advance. But Christian hope is based on the promise of God, and therefore it cannot disappoint. No, it is the anchor of the aged soul, becoming brighter and more enduring as the years pass by, because "He is faithful that promised."

But how may we increase our hope, so as never to let it slip, but to hold it fast with unwavering firmness? There is nothing which will sooner strengthen it than to consider His faithfulness whose promises are hope's anchorage. Has He ever failed to fulfil His engagements? Do not the stars return to their appointed place to a hairbreadth of their time? Have not good men given a unanimous testimony to the fidelity of the covenant-keeping God? He has never suffered His faithfulness to fail - and never will. Our hope, therefore, need not falter, but be strong and very courageous.

LOVE comes last. She is queen of all the graces of the inner life. Love is the passion of self-giving. It never stays to ask what it can afford, or what it may expect to receive, but it is ever shedding forth its perfume, breaking its alabaster boxes, and shedding its heart's blood.

It will pine to death if it cannot give. It must share its possessions. It is prodigal of costliest service. Such love is in the heart of God, and should also be in us, and we may increase it materially by considering one another, and associating with our fellow-believers.

Distance begets coldness and indifference. When we forsake the assembly of our fellow-Christians we are apt to wrap ourselves in the chill mantle of indifference. But when we see others in need, and help them, when we are willing to succour and save, when we discover that there is something attractive in the least loveable, when we feel the glowing sympathy of others - our own love grows by the demands made on it, and by the opportunities of manifestation.

Let us seek earnestly these best gifts, and that we may have them and abound, let us invoke the blessed indwelling of the Lord Jesus, whose entrance brings with it the whole train of sweet Christian graces.

THE THREEFOLD REMONSTRANCE. Go forward! otherwise penalty (verse 26). If a man unwittingly broke Moses' law, he was forgiven; but if he wilfully despised it, he died without mercy. What then can be expected by those who sin wilfully, not against the iron obligations of Sinai, but against the gracious words which distil from the lips of the dying Saviour!

The heart that can turn from the love and blood-shedding of Calvary, and ignore them, and trample them ruthlessly under foot, is so hard, so hopeless, so defiant of the Holy Spirit as to expose itself to the gravest displeasure of God, and can expect no further offering for its sins. There is no sacrifice for the atonement of the sin of rejecting Calvary.

Go forward! otherwise past efforts nullified (verse 32). These Hebrew Christians had suffered keenly on their first entrance into the Christian life. The martyrdom of the saintly Stephen, the great havoc wrought in the Church by Saul of Tarsus, the terrible famines that visited Jerusalem, causing widespread destitution.

They had become even a gazing-stock by reproaches and afflictions. But they had taken joyfully the spoiling of their goods, not shrinking from the ordeal. To go back to Judaism now would annul the advantages which otherwise might have accrued from their bitter experience, would not reap the harvest of their tears, would counterwork the respect with which they were being regarded, and would rob them of the reward which the Lord might give to them, if they only endured to the end. "Cast not away your boldness, which has great recompense of reward."

Go forward! the Lord is at hand (verse 36). Jesus was about to come in the fall of Jerusalem, as He will come ere long to close the present age, and every sign pointed to the speedy destruction of the Jewish polity by the all-conquering might of Rome. How foolish then would it be to return to that which was on the eve of dissolution, to the Temple that would burn to the ground, to sacrifices soon to cease, to a priesthood to be speedily scattered to the winds!

There was only one alternative. Not to go back to certain perdition, to the ruin of all the nobler attributes of the soul, to disgrace and disappointment and endless regret, but to go on through evil and good report, through sorrow and anxiety and blood, until the faithful servant should be vindicated by the Lord's approval, and welcomed into the realms of endless blessedness.

Are we amongst those who go on to the saving of the soul? Here, as so often, the salvation of the soul is viewed as a process.

True, we are in a sense saved when first we turn to the cross and trust the Crucified. But it is only as we keep in the current that streams from the cross, only as we remain in abiding fellowship with the Saviour, only as we submit ourselves habitually to the gracious influences of the divine Spirit, that salvation pervades and heals our whole being. Then the soul may be said to be gained (R.V., margin), i.e., restored to its original type as conceived in the mind of God before He built the dust of the earth into man, and breathed into him the breath of life, and he became a living soul.

CHAPTER 26: FAITH AND ITS EXPLOITS

"Now faith is the substance of things hoped for, the evidence of things not seen." (HEBREWS 11.1).

SOCIETY rests on the faith which man has in man. The workman, toiling through the week for the wage which he believes he will receive, the passenger, procuring a ticket for a distant town, because he believes the statements of the timetables, the sailor steering his bark with unerring accuracy in murky weather, because he believes in the mercantile charts and tables, the entire system of monetary credit, by which vast sums circulate from hand to hand without the use of a single coin - all these are illustrations of the immense importance of faith in the affairs of men.

Nothing, therefore, is more disastrous for an individual or a community than for its credit to be impaired, or its confidence shaken.

There seem to be three necessary preliminaries in order to faith. First, some one must make an engagement or promise. Second, there must be good reason for believing in the integrity and sufficiency of the person by whom the engagement has been made. Third, there follows a comfortable assurance that it will be even so.

In fact, the believer is able to count on the object promised as being not less sure than if it had already come into actual possession. And this latter frame of mind is precisely the one indicated by the writer of this Epistle, when, guided by the Holy Spirit, he affirms that faith is the assurance of things hoped for, the persuasion or conviction of things not seen. In other words, faith is the faculty of realising the unseen.

These three conditions are fulfilled in Christian faith. The same faculty is called into action with respect to the things of God. At the outset we are sure that a Voice has spoken to man from the page of Scripture. Not voices, but a Voice. Next, we are sure that this Speaker is infinitely credible. Our assurance rests on several grounds. We find that His words have ever come true in the experience of past generations. We have seen them accompanied by the introduction of miraculous phenomena, indicating in their beneficence and power the goodness and glory of the Worker. We discover in our own hearts the assent of our moral nature to their evident truth. And for all these reasons we hold that the Voice which speaks deserves our credence.

And therefore, lastly, we calculate on whatever has been promised as surely as if we saw it, and may reckon on it as certainly ours.

Let us emphasise again what has been said. We look on the words which God speaks to us from the Scriptures as being altogether different from any other words which may claim our attention from the lips of men, not only because of the character of the miracles which accompany them, but because they touch us as no other words do, and elicit the spontaneous assent and consent of our moral nature, though sometimes in condemnation of ourselves. That must be the Book of God which so exactly coincides with the best emotions and intuitions of our moral nature; and not of ours only, but of the noblest and best of our race

"The mighty God, the Lord has spoken, and called the earth from the rising of the sun to the going down of the same." And if we are once assured of this, then there is no limit to the restful confidence, which not only counts the promise as credible, but actually begins to enjoy in anticipation the boons they offer.

The maxim of human experience runs thus: 'Seeing is believing'. But with the child of God the reverse is true: 'Believing is seeing'. We are as sure of what God had promised as we would be if we saw it already before our eyes. Our vision could not make us more sure than we are that God loves us, that there is a Father's house with its many mansions, and that some day our mortality is to put on immortality, so as to live forever in a state of existence which is absolutely sinless, sorrowless, and nightless.

Such faith as this is begotten in our souls, primarily by the study of God's Word, appealing, as we have seen, to our moral consciousness, which, as it is more and more developed, is more and more satisfied with the Book which called it into being, and has done so much for its education.

But sometimes faith seems to be given us in respect of some special matter which is not directly indicated in Scripture, but which we feel able to claim, yes, and as we pray and think over it we are still more able to claim it. And when we find such a conviction forming in our hearts, we may be perfectly sure of it. "Whoever will say to this mountain, Be removed, and be cast into the sea, and shall not doubt in his heart, but believe that those things which he says will come to pass, he shall have whatever he says." Thus the child of God may begin to praise for blessings of which there is no outward sign, being as sure of them as though they had risen above the horizon, like the little cloud, no bigger than a man's hand, to Elijah's prayer. "We have the petitions that we desired of Him."

Do you want a greater faith? Then consider the promises, which are its native food! Read the story of God's mighty acts in bygone days. Open your heart to God, that He may shine in with His own revealing presence. Ask Him to give you this wondrous faculty to which nothing is impossible. Put away from you aught which might clash with the growth of your heart in faith and love.

FAITH MAKES MEN GREAT. Run through this roll-call of heroes. You must admit that those whose names are mentioned stand in the first ranks of our race, shining as stars. But their claim to be thus regarded was certainly not natural genius.

Enoch, for instance, and his line, being Sethites, may have been inferior to many of the family of Cain, so far as mere intellectual or artistic attainment went. But his faith lifted him out of the ranks of mediocrity to a species of primacy amongst men. And should faith become the master-principle of your life and mine, it would similarly enlarge and enrich our whole being.

FAITH MIGHTILY AFFECTS OUR ORDINARY HUMAN LIFE. With most men you can determine pretty nearly how they will act in given circumstances. You can enumerate the influences at work, and their value. But you can never be sure in the case of the Christian, because his faith is making real much of which the world around takes no thought whatever.

The tyrant, anxious to save some young Christian confessor, approaches him with flatteries and promises, things that attract the young, and is surprised to find that they have no charm. He then approaches with suffering, obloquy, and death, things that sadden young hearts, and is equally astonished to discover that they cause no alarm. The cause is inexplicable, and is set down to obstinacy; but in point of fact the eyes of the young heart are opened on a world of which the tyrant has formed no conception.

Faith is not careless of time, but more mindful of eternity. Faith does not underrate the power of man, but she magnifies omnipotence. Faith is not callous of present pain, but she weighs it against future joy. Against ill-gotten gains, she puts eternal treasure; against human hate the recompense of reward; against the weariness of the course, the crown of amaranth; against the tears of winter sowing, the shoutings of the autumn sheaves; against the inconvenience of the tent, the permanent city.

None of these men would have lived the noble lives they did, had it not been for the recompense of reward and the gleams given them of the golden city amid the sorrows and straits of their lives.

FAITH IS POSSIBLE TO ALL CLASSES. In this list are women as well as men. Sarah and Rahab, as well as Abraham and Joshua, the widow of Shunem, and the mighty prophet who brought her son back to life, Moses, the student of Egypt's wisdom, Gideon, the husbandman, Isaac, the grazier, Jacob, the shrewd cattle breeder, Barak, the soldier, David, the shepherd, and Samuel, the prophet. Their Occupations and circumstances varied infinitely, but there was not one of them that did not live under the influence of this master-principle. Whatever may be a man's lawful calling, he may abide therein with God, under the influence of faith. Like the fir or pine, faith flourishes in any soil.

FAITH IS CONSISTENT WITH VERY DIFFERENT DEGREES OF KNOWLEDGE. It would be difficult to enumerate more varieties of religious knowledge than are summarised in. this catalogue of names. Abel's idea of sacrifice would differ widely from David's. The degree of acquaintance with God would be much intenser with Moses than Samson. And, compared with the clear views of truth held by these Hebrew Christians, those of the world's grey fathers were but as baskets full of fragments. But, notwithstanding all these differences, the same principle of faith leaped upward from each heart. And the woman who touched the hem of the garment was animated with the same spirit as that which in her sister elicited the wonder of Jesus: "0h woman, great is your faith!"

FAITH CAN MASTER INSUPERABLE DIFFICULTIES. It is difficult to be singular, but faith enabled Abel to offer a more excellent sacrifice than Cain. It is difficult to walk constantly with God, when wickedness is great on the earth, and all flesh has corrupted its way, but it is not impossible, for Enoch walked with God on the very margin of the Flood, and obtained the testimony that he pleased Him.

It is difficult to lead a pilgrim life, and such difficulties would be probably as keenly felt by the patriarchs, but what faith did for them it will do for others. It is difficult, amid the cares of business or public office, to keep the heart fresh, devout, and young, but it is not impossible to faith, which maintained the spirit of patriotism and devotion in the heart of Joseph, though sorely tempted to sink into an Egyptian grandee. It is difficult to face the loss of all things, and the displeasure of the great, but Moses did both, under the spell of faith in the unseen.

There are many difficulties before us all. Stormy seas forbid our passage, frowning fortifications bar our progress, mighty kingdoms defy our power, lions roar against us, fire lights its flaming barricade in our path, the sword, the armies of the alien, mockings, scourgings, bonds, and imprisonment - all these menace our peace, darken our horizon, and try on us their power; but faith has conquered all these before, and it will do as much again.

We will laugh at impossibility, we will tread the shores of the seas, certain they must make us a way, we will enter the dens of wild beasts and the furnaces of flame, sure that they are impotent to injure us, we will escape the edge of the sword, out of weakness become strong, turn to flight armies of aliens, and set at nought all the power of the enemy. And all because we believe in God.

Reckon on God's faithfulness. Look not at the winds and waves, but at His character and will. Get alone with Him, steeping your heart and mind in His precious and exceeding great promises. Be obedient to the utmost limit of your light. Walk in the Spirit, one of whose fruits is faith. So shall you be deemed worthy to join this band, whose names and exploits run over from this page into the chronicles of eternity, and to share their glorious heritage.

CHAPTER 27: STRIPPING FOR THE RACE

"Wherefore, seeing we also are compassed about with so great a cloud of witnesses, let us lay aside every weight, and the sin which does so easily beset us, and let us run with patience the race that is set before us, looking unto Jesus, the author and finisher of our faith." (HEBREWS 12.1-2).

WHEN, in his Egyptian campaign, the Emperor Napoleon was leading his troops through the neighbourhood of the Pyramids, he pointed to those hoary remnants of a great antiquity, and said, "Soldiers, forty centuries look down on you!

Similarly there have been summoned before our thought in the preceding chapter the good and great, the martyrs, confessors, prophets, and kings of the past. We have been led through the corridors of the divine mausoleum, and bidden to read the names and epitaphs of those of whom God was not ashamed.

We have felt our faith grow stronger as we read and pondered the inspiring record, and now, by a single touch, these saintly souls are depicted as having passed from the arena into the crowded tiers, from which to observe the course which we are treading today. They were witnesses to the necessity, nature, and power of faith. They are witnesses also of our lives and struggles, our victories and defeats, our past and present.

And they are compared to a cloud. One of the finest pictures in the world is that of the Madonna de San Sisto at Dresden, which depicts the infant Saviour in the arms of His mother, surrounded by clouds, which attracted no special notice until lately, but when the accumulated dust of centuries was removed, they were found to be composed of myriads of angel faces. Surely this is the thought of the inspired writer when he speaks of "so great a cloud of witnesses."

In some of the more spacious amphitheatres of olden times, the spectators rose in tier above tier to the number of forty or fifty thousand, and to the thought of the combatant as he looked around on this vast multitude of human faces, set in varied and gorgeous colouring, these vast congregations of his race must have appeared like clouds, composed of infinitesimal units, but all making up one mighty aggregate, and bathed in such hues as are cast on the clouds at sunrise or sunset by the level sun.

If before this time these Hebrew Christians had been faltering, and inclined to relinquish their earnestness, they would have been strangely stirred and quickened by the thought that they were living under the close inspection of the spirits of the mighty dead. To us also the same exhortation applies.

THE SPEED OF THE CHRISTIAN LIFE. "Let us run." We must not sit still to be carried by the stream. We must not loiter and linger as children returning from a summer's ramble. We must not even walk as men with measured step. We must run. Nor are we only to run as those who double their pace to an easy trot; we must run as men who run a race. The idea of a race is generally competition. Here it is only concentration of purpose, singleness of aim, intensity.

Life in earnest - that is the idea. But how far do we seem from it! And what a contrast there is between our earnestness in all beside, and in our devotion to God and man! We are willing enough to join in the rush of business competition, in the race for wealth, in the heated discussion of politics, and in social life in the pursuit of pleasure, but, ah! how soon we slacken when it becomes a question of how much we are willing to do for God!

How earnest men are around us! Newton pouring over his problems till the midnight wind sweeps over his pages the ashes of his long-extinguished fire. Reynolds sitting, brush in hand, before his canvas for thirty six hours together, summoning into life forms of beauty that seemed glad to come. Dryden composing in a single fortnight his Ode for St. Cecilia's Day. Buffon dragged from his beloved slumbers to his more beloved studies. And the biographer who records these traits himself rising with the dawn to prepare for the demands of his charge.

In a world like this, and with a theme like ours, we ought not to be languid and supine, but devoted, eager, consumed with a holy love to God, and with a passion for the souls of men. Then would we make progress in the knowledge of the Word of God, and enter into the words of one of the greatest spiritual athletes that ever lived, "This one thing I do . . . I press toward the goal for the prize of the high calling in Christ Jesus."

WE MUST RUN FREE OF WEIGHTS. This speed can only be maintained when we run unencumbered and free. Now, of course we would all admit the necessity of divesting ourselves of sins, but in all our lives there are weights which are not sins.

A sin is that which in its very nature, and always, and by whoever perpetrated, is a transgression of God's law, a violation of God's will. But a weight is something which in itself or to another may be harmless, or even legitimate, but in our own case is a hindrance and an impediment.

Every believer must be left to decide what is his own special weight. We may not judge for one another. What is a weight to one is not so to all. But the Holy Spirit, if He be consulted and asked to reveal the hindrance to the earnestness and speed of the soul's progress in divine things, will not fail to indicate it swiftly and infallibly. And this is the excellence of the Holy Spirit's teaching: it is ever definite.

If you have a general undefined feeling of discouragement, it is probably the work of the great enemy of souls, but if you are aware of some one hindrance and encumbrance which stays your speed, it is almost certainly the work of the divine Spirit, who is leading you to relinquish something which is slackening your progress in the spiritual life.

No man would think of maintaining a high speed encompassed with weights. The lads who run for a prize litter the course with garments flung away in their eager haste. There would be little difficulty in maintaining an intense and ardent spirit if we were more faithful in dealing with the habits and indulgences which cling around us and impede our steps.

Thousands of Christians are like water-logged vessels. They cannot sink, but they are so saturated with inconsistencies and worldliness and permitted evil that they can only be towed with difficulty into the celestial port.

Is there anything in your life which dissipates your energy from holy things, which disinclines you to the practise of prayer and Bible study, which rises before you in your best moments, and produces in you a general sense of uneasiness and disturbance, something which others account harmless, and permit, and in which you once saw no cause for anxiety, but which you now look on with a feeling of self-condemnation? It is likely enough a weight.

Is there anything within the circle of your consciousness concerning which you have to argue with yourself, or which you do not care to investigate, treating it as a bankrupt treats his books into which he has no desire to enter, or as a votary of pleasure treats the first symptoms of decaying vitality which he seeks to conceal from himself? We so often allow in ourselves things which we would be the first to condemn in others.

We frequently find ourselves engaged in discovering ingenious reasons why a certain course which would be wrong in others is justifiable in ourselves. All such things may be considered as weights. It may be a friendship which is too engrossing, a habit which is sapping away our energy as the taproot does the fruit bearing powers of a tree, a pursuit, an amusement, a pastime, a system of reading, a method of spending time, too fascinating and too absorbing, and therefore harmful to the soul - which is tempted to walk when it should run, and to loiter when it should haste.

But, you ask, Is it not a sign of weakness, and will it not tend to weakness, always to be relinquishing these and similar things? Surely, you cry, the life will become impoverished and barren when it is stripped in this way of its precious things.

Not so. It is impossible to renounce anything at the bidding of the inner life without adding immensely to its strength; for it grows by surrender, and waxes strong by sacrifice. And for every unworthy object which is forsaken there follows an immediate enrichment of the spirit, which is the sufficient and unvarying compensation.

The athlete gladly foregoes much that other men value, and which is pleasant to himself, because his mind is intent on the prize, and he considers that he will be amply repaid for all the hardships of training if he be permitted to bear it away, though it be a belt he will never wear, or a cup he will never use.

How much more gladly should we be prepared to relinquish all that hinders our attainment, not of the uncertain bauble of the athlete, but the certain reward, the incorruptible crown, the smile and "well-done" of our Lord!

There is an old Dutch picture of a little child dropping a cherished toy from its hands, and, at first sight, its action seems unintelligible, until, at the corner of the picture, the eye is attracted to a white dove winging its flight toward the emptied outstretched hands. Similarly we are prepared to forego a good deal when once we catch sight of the spiritual acquisitions which beckon to us. And this is the true way to reach consecration and surrender.

Do not ever dwell on the giving-up side, but on the receiving side. Keep in mind the meaning of the old Hebrew word for consecration, to fill the hand. There will not be much trouble in getting men to empty their hands of wood, hay, and stubble if they see that there is a chance of filling them with the treasures which gleam from the faces or lives of others, or which call to them from the page of Scripture.

The world pities us, because it sees only what we give up, but it would hold its sympathy if it could also see how much we receive "good measure, pressed down, and running over given into our bosoms."

WE MUST LAY ASIDE BESETTING SIN. "Let us lay aside the sin which does so closely cling to us" (R.V.). We often refer to these words. No sentence of the Bible is more often on our lips. But do we not misquote them in divorcing them from their context? We should read them as part of the great argument running through the previous chapter, and of which they are the culmination and brilliant climax.

That argument has been devoted to the theme of faith. Case after case has been adduced of the exploits of the heroes of Hebrew story; and it has been shown that in each faith was the secret motive and the sufficient power.

The close connection between that glowing panegyric and the opening words of the following chapter is shown by the word "Wherefore," which even defies the wanton intrusion of the division forced upon us in our English version.

And surely it is most natural to hold that the sin which so closely clings to us is nothing else than the sin of unbelief, which is the opposite pole to the faith so highly eulogised.

If that be a correct exegesis, it sheds new light on unbelief. It is no longer an infirmity, it is a sin. Men sometimes carry about their doubts, as beggars a deformed or sickly child, to excite the sympathy of the benevolent. But surely there is a kind of unbelief which should not meet with sympathy, but rebuke. It is sin which needs to be repented of as sin, to be resisted as sin, and to receive as sin the cleansing of Christ.

Unbelief may, as in the case of Thomas, spring from intellectual and constitutional difficulties. But these will not lead the soul to vaunt itself as surpassing others in insight, or to relinquish the society of others with happier constitutions, or, above all, to forego the habit of secret prayer. It will rather induce a temper of mind the very opposite of that self-confident, arrogant spirit which prevails so much in the unbelievers of our time.

But much unbelief springs from moral causes. The soul gets wrong with God, and says that it is not sure whether there is a God. The windows are allowed to be covered with grime, and then it doubts whether the sun is shining. The faculties of the inner life are clogged with neglect, and refuse to do their appointed office in revealing the spiritual and the unseen.

We would be wiser if we dealt with much of the unbelief of our time as a disease of the spiritual life, rather than of the intellectual. Its source is largely moral. Do not set agnostics to study evidences, but show them that their temper of heart is the true cause of their darkness and unbelief.

God has given each of us powers of discerning His truth, which will certainly perceive and love it, and where the reverse is the case, it is often due to some moral obliquity, to some beam in the eye, to some secret indulgence, which is destructive of all spiritual perception.

Put away known sin. Read the Bible, even though you doubt its inspiration. Wait. Pray. Live up to all the light you have. And unbelief will drop away as the old leaves from the evergreens in spring.

There will, of course, be difficulties in all our lives to impede our heavenward progress: difficulties from the opposition of our foes, difficulties from within our own hearts. We shall need patience and long forbearance as we tread our appointed track. But there are two sources of comfort open to us.

Let us remember that the course is set before us by our heavenly Father, who therefore knows all its roughness and straitness, and will make all grace abound toward us, sufficient for our need. To do His will is rest and heaven.

Let us "look off unto Jesus." Away from past failure and success, away from human applause and blame, away from the gold pieces scattered on the path, and the flowers that line either side.

Do not look now and again, but acquire the habit of looking always, so that it shall become natural to look up from every piece of daily work, from every room, however small, from every street, however crowded, to His dear, calm, sweet face, just as the sojourner on the northern shores of Geneva's lake is constantly prone to look up from any book or work on which the attention may have been engaged, to behold the splendour and glory of the noble range of snow-capped summits on the further shores. And if it seems hard to acquire this habitual attitude, trust the Holy Spirit to form it in your soul.

Above all, remember that where you tread, there your Lord once trod, combating your difficulties and sorrows, though without sin, and ere long you shall be where He is now. Keep your eye fixed, then, on Him as He stands to welcome and reward you, and struggle through all, animated by His smile, and attracted to His side, and you will find weights and unbelief dropping off almost insensibly and of themselves.

This is the only way by which souls can be persuaded. Argue with them, urge them, try to force them - and they will cling the closer to the encumbrances which are clogging their steps. But present to them Jesus in the beauty and attractiveness of His person and work, and there will be a natural loosening of impediments, as the snow which had been bending the leaves to the earth drops away when the sun begins to shine.

And God never takes aught from us, without giving us something better. He removes the symbol, to give us the reality; breaks the type, to give the substance, releases us from the natural and human, to give us the divine. Oh, trust Him, soul, and dare to let go, that you may take, to be stripped, that you may become clothed!

CHAPTER 28: CHASTISEMENT

Whom the Lord loves He chastens, and scourges every son whom He receives." (HEBREWS 12.6).

It is hardly possible to suppose that any will read these lines who have not drunk of the bitter cup of affliction. Some may have even endured a great fight of afflictions. Squadron after squadron has been drawn up in array, and broken its regiments on the devoted soul.

It has come to us in different forms, but in one form or another it has come to us all. Perhaps our physical strength and health have been weakened in the way, or we have been racked with unutterable anguish in mind or body; or have been obliged to see our beloved slowly slipping from the grasp of our affection, which was condemned to stand paralysed and helpless by.

In some cases, affliction has come to us in the earning of our daily bread, which has been procured with difficulty and pain, whilst care has never been long absent from our hearts, or want from our homes. In others, homes which were as full of merry voices as the woods in spring of sweet-voiced choristers are empty and silent. Ah, how infinite are the shades of grief! How extended the gamut of pain! How many can cry with the Psalmist, "All Your waves and Your billows are gone over me!

We can see clearly the reason of all this suffering. The course of nature is out of joint. Man's sin has put not himself only, but the whole course of nature into collision with the will and law of God, so that it groans and travails in its pains. Selfishness has also alienated man from his fellows, inciting him to amass all that he can lay hands on for himself, oblivious to the bitter sufferings of those around him, and careless of their woes. Whilst behind the whole course of nature there is the incessant activity of malignant spirits, who, as in the case of Job, may be plotting against us, revelling in any mischief, which, for some great reasons, they are permitted to work to our hurt.

There are different ways in which affliction may be borne. Some despise it (verse 5). They refuse to acknowledge any reason in themselves for its infliction. They reject the lesson it was designed to teach. They harden themselves in stoical indifference, resolving to bear it with defiant and desperate courage.

Some faint under it (verse 5). They become despondent and dispirited, or lose heart and hope. Like Pliable, they are soon daunted, and get out of the Slough of Despond with as little cost as possible to themselves, or, like Timorous and Mistrust, turn back from the lion's roar.

We ought to be in subjection, lifting the cup meekly and submissively to our lips, calmly and trustfully saying "Amen" to every billow and wave, lovingly trying to learn the lesson written on the page of trial, and bowing ourselves as the reeds of the river's edge to the sweeping hurricane of trial.

But this, though the only true and safe course, is by no means an easy one. Subjection in affliction is only possible when we can see in it the hand of the Father of spirits (verse 9).

So long as we look at the second causes, at men or things, as being the origin and source of our sorrows, we shall be filled alternately with burning indignation and hopeless grief. But when we come to understand that nothing can happen to us except as our Father permits, and that, though our trials may originate in some lower source, yet they become God's will for us as soon as they are permitted to reach us through the defence of His environing presence, then we smile through our tears, we kiss the dear hand that uses another as its rod, we realise that each moment's pain originates in our Father's heart, and we are at rest.

Judas may seem to mix the cup, and put it to our lips, but it is nevertheless the cup which our Father gives us to drink, and shall we not drink it? Much of the anguish passes away from life's trials as soon as we discern our Father's hand. Then affliction becomes chastisement. There is a great difference between these two.

Affliction may come from a malignant and unfriendly source, chastisement is the work of the Father, yearning over His little children, desiring to eliminate from their characters all that is unlovely and unholy, and to secure in them entire conformity to His character and will.

But, before you can appropriate the comfort of these words, let me earnestly ask you, my reader, whether you are a child? None are children in the sense of which we are speaking now, save those who have been born into the divine family by regeneration, through the grace of the Holy Spirit. Of this birth, faith is the sure sign and token, for it is written: "Those that believe on his name are born, not of blood, nor of the will of the flesh, nor of the will of man, but of God."

Are you a child? Does the Spirit witness with your spirit that you are born of God? Can you look up into his face and cry, "Abba, Father"? If so, you are surrounded by your Father's tender, loving care. Nothing can reach you without passing through the cordon of His protection.

If, therefore, affliction does lay its rough hand upon your arm, arresting you, then be sure that it must first have obtained permission from One Who loves you infinitely, and Who is willing to expose both you and Himself to pain because of the vast profit on which He has set His heart.

All chastisement has a Purpose. There is nothing so absolutely crushing in sorrow as to feel one's self drifting at the mercy of some chance wave, sweeping forward to an unknown shore. But a great calm settles down upon us when we realise that life is a schoolhouse, in which we are being taught by our Father Himself, Who sets our lessons as He sees we require them.

The drill-sergeant has a purpose in every exercise, the professor of music an object in every scale, the farmer an end in every method of husbandry. "He does not thresh fitches with a sharp threshing instrument, neither is a cartwheel turned about upon cummin, but the fitches He permits us to feel. There is nothing fortuitous or empirical or capricious in His dealings with his own.

The purposes which chastisement subserves are very various. Of course we know that the penalty of our sins has been laid on the head of our great Substitute, and that, therefore, we are forever relieved from their penal consequences. But though that is so, yet often chastisement follows on our wrongdoing. Not that we expiate the wrongdoing by suffering, but that we may be compelled to regard it in its true light.

Amid the pain we suffer we are compelled to review our past. The carelessness, the unwatchfulness, the prayerlessness which have been working within us pass slowly before our minds. We see where we had been going astray for long months or years. We discover how deeply and incessantly we had been grieving God's Holy Spirit. We find that an alienation had been widening the breach between God and our souls, which, if it had proceeded further, must have involved moral ruin. Perhaps we never see our true character until the light dies off the landscape, and the clouds overcast the sky, and the wind rises moaningly about the house of our life.

Times of affliction lead to heart-searchings, and we become increasingly aware of sins of which we had hardly thought at all. And even though the offence may be confessed and put away, so long as affliction lasts there is a subdued temper of heart and mind, which is most favourable to religious growth.

We cannot forget our sin so long as the stroke of the Almighty lies on our soul, and we are compelled to maintain a habit of holy watchfulness against its recurrence.

It is also in affliction that we learn that fellowship with the sufferings of Christ and that sympathy for others which are so lovely in true Christians.

That is not the loftiest type of character which, like the Chinese pictures, has no background of shadow. Even Christ could only learn obedience by the things that He suffered, or become a perfect High-Priest by the ordeal of temptation. And how little can we enter into the inner depths of His soul, unless we tread the shadowed paths, or lie prostrate in the secluded glades of Gethsemane! We who attempt to assuage the griefs of mankind must ourselves be acquainted with grief, and become men of sorrows.

Be sure, then, that not one moment's pain is given you to bear that could have been dispensed with. Each has been the subject of divine consideration before permitted to come, and each will be removed directly its needed mission is fulfilled.

Special discipline is evidence of special love (verse 6). It costs us much less to fling our superfluities on those we love than to cause them pain. Indulgence is a sign not of intense but of slender love. The heart that really and wisely loves will bear the pain of causing pain, will incur the risk of being misjudged, will not flinch from misrepresentation and reproach, from all of which a less affection would warily shrink.

It is because our Father loves us that He chastens us. He would not take so much trouble over us if we were not dear to His heart. It is because we are sons that He sets Himself to scourge us. But oh, how much He suffers as He wields that scourge of small cords! Yet, hail each blow; for each sting and smart cries to you that you are being received into the inner circle of love.

When suppliants for His healing help came to our Lord, for the most part He hastened to their side. But on one occasion He lingered yet two days in the place where He was. He dared to face the suspicion of neglect and the loving impeachment of bereaved love, because He loved Martha and her sister and Lazarus. He loved them too much to be satisfied with doing small things for them, or revealing only fragments of His great glory. He longed to enrich them with his precious revelation of resurrection life.

But His end could only be reached at the cost of untold sorrow, even to death. Lazarus must die, and lie for two days in the grave, before His mightiest miracle could be wrought. And so he let the thundercloud break on the home He loved, that He might be able to flash on it light which broke into a rainbow of prismatic glory.

If you are signally visited with suffering, such as you cannot connect with persistence in carelessness or neglect, then take it that you are one of Heaven's favourites. It is not, as men think, the child of fortune and earthly grace, dowered with gifts in prodigal profusion, who is best beloved of God, but oftenest the child of poverty and pain and misfortune and heartbreak. "If you be without chastisement, whereof all are partakers, then you are bastards and not sons." Oh, you who escape the rod, begin seriously to ask whether indeed you are born again!

Pain is fraught with precious results. (verses 10-11). " Not joyous but grievous: nevertheless afterward." How full of meaning is the "afterward." Who shall estimate the hundredfold of blessing from each moment of pain?

The Psalms are crystallised tears. The Epistles were in many cases written in prison. The greatest teachers of mankind have learned their most helpful lessons in sorrow's school. The noblest characters have been forged in a furnace. Acts which will live forever, masterpieces of art and music and literature, have originated in ages of storm and tempest and heart-rending agony. And so also is it with our earthly discipline. The ripest results are sorrow-born. "The path of sorrow, and that path alone, Leads to the land where sorrow is unknown."

Holiness is the product of sorrow, when sanctified by the grace of God. Not that sorrow necessarily makes us holy, because that is the prerogative of the divine Spirit, and, as a matter of fact, many sufferers are hard and complaining and unlovely. But that sorrow predisposes us to turn from the distractions of earth to receive those influences of the grace of God which are most operative where the soul is calm and still, sitting in a veiled and darkened room, whilst suffering plies body or mind. Who of us does not feel willing to suffer, if only this precious result shall accrue, that we may be "partakers of His holiness" ?

Fruit is another product (verse 11). Where, think you, does the Husbandman of souls most often see the fruit He loves so well, and hear the tones of deepest trust? Not where His gifts are most profuse, but where they are most meagre. Not within the halls of successful ambition or satiated luxury, but in cottages of poverty, and rooms dedicated to ceaseless pain. Genial almost to a miracle is the soil of sorrow. Necessary beyond all count is the pruning-knife of pain.

Count, if you will, the precious kinds of fruit. There is patience, which endures the Father's will, and trust that sees the Father's hand behind the rough disguise, and peace, that lies still, content with the Father's plan, and righteousness, that conforms itself to the Father's requirements, and love, that clings more closely than ever to the Father's heart; and gentleness,hich deals leniently with others, because of what we have learned of ourselves.

Nor is it for very long. Jesus, Who endured the cross and shame and spitting, is now set down on the right hand of the throne of God. Ere long we too shall come out of the great tribulation, to sit by His side. Every tear kissed away, every throb of anguish stayed, every memory of pain allayed by God's anodyne of bliss. The results will be ours forever.

But sorrow and sighing, which may have been our daily comrades to the gates of the celestial city, will flee away as we step across its threshold, unable to exist in that radiant glory. "And God shall wipe away all tears from their eyes; and there shall be no more death, neither sorrow nor crying; neither shall there be any more pain." "For I reckon that the sufferings of this present time are not worthy to be compared with the glory which shall be revealed in us." "For our light affliction, which is but for a moment, works for us a far more exceeding and eternal weight of glory." "Wherefore lift up the hands that hang down, and the feeble knees."

CHAPTER 29: THE IDEAL LIFE

"Follow peace with all men, and holiness, without which no man shall see the Lord, looking diligently lest any man fail of the grace of God, lest any root of bitterness springing up trouble you, and thereby many be defiled." (HEBREWS 12.14-15).

How beautiful and solemn are these words, like the swelling cadence of heaven's own music. Evidently they do not emanate from this sorrow-stricken and warring world, they are one of the laws of the kingdom of heaven, intended to mould and fashion our life on earth.

It is quite likely that those who elect to obey them may not achieve name and fame amongst men, but they will win something infinitely better - the beatitude of blessedness, the smile of the Saviour, and the vision of God.

There are souls among us of whom the world is not worthy, yet for whom the world, when it catches sight of them, prepares its bitterest venom, who have withdrawn their interest from the ambitions and schemes, the excitements and passions of their fellows, and who live a retired life, hidden with Christ in God, content to be unknowing and unknown, eager only to please God, to know Him, or rather to be known of Him, and to preserve the perfect balance of their nature with Him, as its centre and pivot and final cause. Such souls, perhaps, will best understand the infinite meaning and beauty of these deep and blessed words.

THERE IS OUR ATTITUDE TOWARD GOD. " Follow after holiness." In the Revised Version this is rendered sanctification." And this in turn is only a Latin equivalent for "setting apart ", as Sinai among mountains, the Sabbath among the days of the week, the Levites among the Jews, and the Jews among the nations of the earth.

But after all there is a deeper thought. Why were people, places, and things set apart? Was it not because God was there? He came down in might and glory on Sinai, therefore they needed to set bounds around its lower declivities. He chose to rest on the seventh day from all His work, therefore it was hallowed and sanctified. He selected the Jews to be His peculiar people, and the Levites to be His priests, therefore they were isolated from all beside. He appeared to Moses in the bush, glowing with the light of the Shekinah, therefore the spot was holy ground, and the shepherd needed to bare his feet. In other words, it is the presence of God which makes holy.

There is only one Being in all the universe who is really holy. Holiness is the attribute of His nature, and of His nature only. We can never be holy apart from God. But when God enters the spirit of man, He brings holiness with Him. No, the presence of God in man is holiness.

A room or public building may be full of delicious sunlight. But that sunlight is not the property of the room. It does not belong to it. You cannot congratulate it upon its possession. For when the shadows of evening gather, and curtain the face of the sun, the chamber is as dark as possible. It is light only so long as the sun dwells in it.

So the human spirit has no holiness apart from God. Holiness is not a perquisite or property or attribute to which any of us can lay claim. It is the indwelling of God's light and glory within us. He is the holy man in whom God dwells. He is the holier in whom God dwells more fully. He is the holiest who, however poor his intellect and mean his earthly lot, is most possessed and filled by the presence of God through the Holy Spirit. We need not wonder at the Apostle addressing believers as saints, when he was able to say of them: "Your body is the temple of the Holy Spirit, which is in you" (1 Corinthians 3.16; 6.19).

Why, then, does the sacred writer bid us "follow after holiness," as though it were an acquisition? Because, though holiness is the infilling of man's spirit by the Spirit of God, yet there are certain very important conditions to be observed by us if we would secure and enjoy that blessed gift.

Give self no quarter. It is always asserting itself in one or other of its Protean shapes. Do not expect to be rid of it. Even if you say you have conquered it, then it lurks beneath the smile of your self-complacency. It may show itself in religious pride, in desire to excel in virtue, in the satisfaction with which we hear ourselves remarked for our humility.

It will need incessant watchfulness, because where self is there God cannot come. He will not share His glory with another. When we are settling down to slumber, we may expect the cry, "Your enemy is upon you", for it will invade our closets and our places of deepest retirement.

It is impossible to read the Epistles of the Apostle Peter without being impressed with the solemn and awful character of the Christian life, the constant need of watchfulness, the urgency for diligence, self-restraint, and self-denial. Oh for this holy sensitiveness! always exercising the self-watch, never sparing ourselves, merciful to others because so merciless to self, continually exercising ourselves to preserve a conscience void of offence toward God and men.

Yield to God. He is ever seeking the point of least resistance in our natures. Help Him to find it, and when found, be sure to let Him have His blessed way. "Whatever he says to you, do it." Work out what God works in. Translate the thoughts of God into the vernacular of daily obedience. Be as plastic to His touch as clay in the hands of the potter, so that you may realise every ideal which is in His heart.

Be not as the horse and mule, but let your mouth be tender to every motion of the divine purpose concerning you. And if you find it difficult to maintain this attitude, be sure to tell your difficulty to the Holy Spirit, and trust Him to keep your heart steadfast and unmoveable, fixed and obedient.

Take time to it. "Follow after." This habit is not to be acquired in a bound or at a leap. It can be formed in its perfection only after years of self-discipline and watchful self-culture. To abide ever in Christ, to yield to God, to keep all the windows of the nature open toward His gracious infilling, to turn naturally to Him, and first, amid peril and temptations, in all times of sorrow and trial, this is not natural, but it may become as second nature by habitual diligence.

But it must necessarily be the work of time ere the sense of effort ceases and the soul naturally and spontaneously turns to God "in every hour of waking thought." And if we are to acquire this blessed and perpetual attitude of soul, we must take time to acquire it, as to acquire aught else which is really precious. It must be no by-play, nor the work of off or leisure hours, nor a pastime, but the serious object of life, the purpose which shall thread all the varied beads of life's chain, and give a beautiful unity to all.

To such a character there shall be the vision of God. "Blessed are the pure in heart; for they shall see God."

Had you been beside Moses during his forty days in the heart of the cloud, when he saw God face to face, you would not have seen him if you had not been holy. Had you stood beside the martyr Stephen when he beheld the glory of God, and the Son of man standing beside Him, your eyes would have discerned nothing if you had not been holy. Yes, if it were possible for you without holiness to pass within the pearly gate, you would not see the sheen, as it were, of sapphire, you would carry with you your own circumference of darkness, and the radiant vision would vanish as you approached. "Without holiness no man shall see the Lord."

The heart has eyes as well as the head, and for want of holiness these become seriously impaired, so that the wise in their own conceits see not, whilst those who are simple, humble, and pure in heart behold the hidden and prepared things of God.

The one condition for seeing God in His Word, in nature, in daily life, and in closet-fellowship, is holiness of heart wrought there by His own indwelling. Follow after holiness as men pursue pleasure; as the athlete runs for the prize, as the votary of fashion follows in the wake of the crowd.

THERE IS OUR ATTITUDE TOWARD MEN. " Follow after peace." The effect of righteousness is always peace. If you are holy, you will be at peace. Peace is broken by sin, but the holy soul takes sin instantly to the Blood. Peace is broken by temptation, but the holy soul has learned to put Christ between itself and the first breath of the tempter. Peace is broken by care, dissatisfaction, and unrest; but the Lord stands around the holy soul, as do the mountains around Jerusalem, which shield off the cruel winds, and collect the rain which streams down their broad sides to make the dwellers in the valleys rejoice and sing. Others may be fretful and feverish, the subjects of wild alarms, but there is perfect peace to the soul which has God and is satisfied.

When a man is full of the peace of God, he will naturally become a son of peace. He will follow after peace with them that call on the Lord out of a pure heart (2 Timothy 2.22). He will endeavour to keep the unity of the Spirit in the bond of peace (Ephesians 4.3). He will sow harvests of peace as he makes peace (James 3. 18). All his epistles, like those of the great Apostle, will breathe benedictions of peace, and his entrance to a home will seem like a living embodiment of the ancient form of benediction. 'Peace be to this house'. He will have a wonderful power of calling out responses from like-minded men, but where that is not the case, his peace, white-robed and dove-winged, shall come back to him again.

But there must be a definite following after peace. The temperaments of some are so trying. They are so apt to look at things in a wrong light, to put misconstructions on harmless actions, and to stand out on trifles. Hence the need of endeavour and patience and watchfulness, that we may exercise a wholesome influence as peacemakers.

Avoid becoming a party to a quarrel. It takes two to make a quarrel, never be one of those. A soft answer will often turn away wrath, and where it does not, yield before the wrongdoer, give place to wrath, let it expend itself unhindered by your resistance. It will soon have vented itself, to be succeeded by shame, penitence, and regret.

If opposed to the malice of men, do not avenge yourselves. Our cause is more God's than it is our own. It is for Him to vindicate us, and He will. He may permit a temporary cloud to rest on us for some wise purpose, but ultimately He will bring out our righteousness as the light, and our judgment as the noonday.

The non-resistance of evil is the dear teaching of Christ (Matthew 5.39; Romans 12.19; 1 Peter 2.21). Stand up for the true, the holy, the good, at all costs, but think very little of standing up for your own rights. What are your rights? Are you anything better than a poor sinner who has forfeited all? You deserve to be treated much worse than you were ever treated at the worst. Leave God to vindicate you.

Do not give cause of offence. If you are aware of certain susceptibilities on the part of others, where they may be easily wounded and irritated, avoid touching them, if you can do so without being a traitor to God's holy truth. And if your brother has any true bill against you, rest not day nor night, tarry not even at the footstool of divine mercy, but go to him forthwith, and seek his forgiveness, and make ample restitution, that he may have no cause of reproach against your professions, or against your Lord (Matthew 5.23).

Oh for more of His peace! - in the face never crossed by impatience, in the voice never rising above gentle tones, in the manner never excited or morose, in the gesture still and restful, which acts as oil poured over the raging billows of the sea when they foam around the bulwarks of the ship and are suddenly quelled.

THERE IS OUR ATTITUDE TOWARD OUR FELLOW CHRISTIANS. "Looking diligently lest any man fail of the grace of God." It is a beautiful provision that love to a common Lord attracts us into the fellowship of His disciples, and as no individual life truly develops in solitariness, so no Christian is right or healthy who isolates himself from the communion of saints. But we go not there only for selfish gratification, but that we may look after one another, not leaving it to the officers of the host, but each doing our own share.

There are three dangers. The laggards. This is the meaning of "fail." The idea is borrowed from a party of travellers, some of whom lag behind, as in the retreat from Moscow, to fall a prey to Cossacks, wolves, or the awful sleep. Let us who are in the front ranks, strong and healthy, go back to look after the weaklings who loiter to their peril.

The root of bitterness. There may be some evil root lurking in some heart, hidden now, but which will bear a terrible harvest of misery to many. So was it in Israel once, when Achan conceived thoughts of covetousness, and brought evil on himself, and mourning on the host whose defeat he had brought about. If we can discover the presence of such roots of bitterness, let us, with much searching of our own souls, humility, and prayer, root them out ere they can spring up to cause trouble.

The profane and earthly-minded. Of these Esau is the type, "who for one morsel of meat sold his birthright." Alas are there not many such? For one momentary gratification of the flesh, they forfeit not their salvation perhaps (we are not told that even Esau forfeited that), but their power to lead, to teach, to receive and hand on blessing to the Church.

Are any such reading these words? Let them beware! Such choices are sometimes irrevocable. So was it with Esau. He wept and cried like some trapped animal, but he could not alter the destiny he had made for himself.

The words "place for repentance" do not refer to his personal salvation, but to the altering of the decision which he had made as a young man, and which his father ratified. He could not undo it. What he had written, he had written. And so there may come a time when you would give everything you possess to have again the old power of blessing and helping your fellows, but you will find that for one moment's sensual gratification, the blessed prerogative has slipped from your grasp, never, never, never to return. Wherefore, let us eagerly and diligently look both to ourselves and our fellow-believers in the Church of God.

CHAPTER 30: SINAI AND SION

"YOU are come to Mount Sion, and to the city of the living God, . . . and to an innumerable company of angels, to the general assembly and church of the firstborn, . . and to God the Judge of all, and to the spirits of just men made perfect, and to Jesus, and to the blood of sprinkling, that speaks better things than that of Abel. " (HEBREWS 12.22-24).

To how great splendour had these Hebrew Christians been accustomed - marble courts, throngs of white-robed Levites, splendid vestments, the state and pomp of symbol, ceremonial, and choral psalm! And to what a contrast were they reduced - a meeting in some hall or school, with the poor, afflicted, and persecuted members of a despised and hated sect!

It was indeed a change, and the inspired writer knew it well, and in these magnificent words, the sublime consummation and crown of his entire argument, he sets himself to show that, for every single item they had renounced, they had become possessed of a spiritual counterpart, a reality, an eternal substance, which was compensation told over a thousand times.

"You are come." He refuses to admit the thought of it being a future experience, reserved for some high day, when the heavenly courts shall be thronged by the populations of redeemed and glorified spirits.

That there will be high days of sacred festivity in that blessed state is clear from the Apocalypse of the beloved Apostle. But it is to none of them that these words allude. Mark that present tense, "You are come." Persecuted, weary, humiliated, these Hebrew Christians had already come to Mount Sion, to the city of the living God, and to the festal throngs of the redeemed. That they saw not these by the eye, and could not touch them by the hand of sense, was no reason for doubting that they had come to these glorious realities.

And what was true of them is true of each reader of these lines who is united to the Lord Jesus by a living faith.

WE BELONG TO MOUNT SION. "You are not come to the mount that might not be touched and that burned with fire, . . . but you are come to Mount Sion." At the bidding of these two words two mountains rise before us. First, Sinai stern and naked, rifted by tempest, cleft by earthquake, the centre and focus of the vast sandstone passages which conducted the pilgrim host, stage above stage, until it halted at its foot.

But, grand as Sinai was by nature, it must have been grander far on that memorable day in which all elements of terror seemed to converge. There was the flash of the forked lightning out of the blackness of the brooding clouds. There was the darkness of midnight, the peal of thunder, the reverberations of which ran in volumes of sound along those resounding corridors, the whirlwind of tempest, and the voice of words which they entreated they might not hear any more.

And all was done to teach the people the majesty, the spirituality, and the holiness of God. The result was terror, struck into the hearts of sinners, trembling at the contrast between the greatness and holiness of God and their own remembered murmurings and shortcomings. Even Moses said: "I exceedingly fear and quake."

In contrast with this stands Mount Sion, the grey old rock on which stood the palace of David and the Temple of God - sites sacred to Jewish thought for holy memories and divine associations.

"The Lord has chosen Sion, He has desired it for His habitation. This is My rest forever. Here will I dwell, for I have desired it." To the pious Jew, Mount Sion was the joy of the whole earth, the mountain of holiness, the city of the Great King. Her palaces, grey with age, were known to be the home and haunt of God. The very aspect of the hoary hills must strike panic into the heart of her foes. And her sons walked proudly around her ramparts, telling her towers, marking her bulwarks, considering her palaces, whilst fathers told to their children the stories of her glory which in their boyhood they too had received (Psalm 58.).

The counterpart of this city is ours still, ours forever. The halo of glory has faded off those ancient stones, and has passed on to rest on the true city of God, of which the foundations are Righteousness, the walls Peace, and the gates Praise, which rises beyond the mists and clouds of time, in the light that shines not from the sun or moon, but from the face of God.

In other words, somewhere in this universe there is a holy society of souls, pure and lovely, the elite of the family of man, gathered in a home which the hand of man has never built, and the sin of man has never soiled. Its walls are jasper, its gates pearl. Into it nothing can enter that defiles or works abomination, and deals in lies.

The patriarchs caught sight of that city in their pilgrimage. It gleamed before their vision, beckoning them ever forward, and forbidding their return to the country from which they had come out. And the Seer of Patmos beheld it descending from God out of heaven, bathed in the divine glory.

To that city we have come. It has come down into our hearts. Day by day we walk its streets, we live in its light, we breathe its atmosphere, we enjoy its rights. We have no counterpart in our experience of Mount Sinai, with its thunder and terror, but, thank God, we have the reality of Mount Sion, with its blessed and holy privileges.

Sinai is the law, temporary and intermediate, Sion, the Gospel, eternal and abiding. Sinai is full of human resolutions and vows, made to be broken, Sion is the election of grace. Sinai is terrible with the thunder of law, Sion is tender with the appeals of the love of the heart of God.

WE BELONG TO A GREAT FESTAL THRONG. The converted Jew might miss the vast crowds that gathered at the annual feasts, when the tribes of the Lord went up, whilst kinsfolk and acquaintance took sweet counsel together, as they went to the house of God in company.

But, to the opened eye of faith, the rooms where they knelt in worship were as full of bright and festal multitudes as the mountain of old was full of horses and chariots of fire. And these are for us also.

There is an innumerable company of angels. Myriads. A thousand thousands minister to our Lord, ten thousand times ten thousand stand before Him. When, therefore, the saintly spirit ascends the altar steps of true devotion, it passes through a vast host of sympathetic spirits, all of whom are devoted to the same Master, and are joining in the same act of worship. Listen! Do you not hear the voice of many angels around the throne as you draw near?

There is also the general assembly and Church of the first-born. We meet the Church of the redeemed each time we sincerely worship God. We may belong to some small section of the visible Church, unrecognised and unknown by the great bulk of our fellow-believers. We may be isolated from all outward fellowship and communion with the saints, imprisoned in the sick-chamber, or self-banished to some lone spot for the sake of the Gospel, but nothing can exclude us from living communion with saintly souls of all communions and sects and denominations and names.

Your name may be written on no communicants' roll, or church register. But is it written in the Lamb's Book of Life in heaven? If so, then rejoice! This is more important than if the spirits were subject to you.

And, remember, whenever you worship God you are ascending the steps of the true temple, in company with vast hosts of souls, whether on this side or on the other of the veil of sense. Neither life nor death nor rite nor church order can divide those who, because they are one with Christ, are forever one with each other.

There are also the spirits of just men made perfect. If the former phrase rather speaks of the New Testament believers, this may be taken to describe the Old Testament saints. Or, if the one designates those who are still serving God on earth, the other probably refers to those who have passed into the presence of God, and have attained their consummation and bliss.

Who can be lonely and desolate, who can bemoan the past, who can disparage the present, when once the spirit is able to realise that rejoicing company, in earth and heaven, circling around the Saviour as planets around the central sun, and sending in tides and torrents of love and worship? Yes, who can forbear to sing, as the ear detects the mighty harmonies of every creature which is in heaven, and on the earth, and under the earth, saying, "Blessing, and honour, and glory, and power, be to Him Who sits on the throne, and to the Lamb forever."

WE ARE COME TO THE BLOOD OF JESUS. We would not dare to approach the august Judge of all, were it not for the Mediator between God and men, Jesus Christ the righteous. Nor would He avail for His chosen work, unless He had shed His most precious blood, which has ratified the new covenant, and cleansed away our sins, and now ever avails to sprinkle us from an evil conscience, removing each stain of guilt so soon as the soul confesses and seeks forgiveness, with tears of penitence and words of faith.

It speaks better things than Abel's. That was the blood of martyrdom, this of sacrifice. That a curse, as it cries from the ground, this only pleads for mercy. That pronounced wrath, this proclaims reconciling love. That led to punishment which branded the murderer, this issues in salvation. That was unto death, this is unto life.

All spilled blood has a cry. Listen to the cry of the blood of Jesus. It speaks to man for God. It speaks to God for man. It tells us that there is no condemnation, no wrath, no judgment, because the thunderstorm broke and exhausted itself on Calvary. And when we go to our Father, it pleads for us from the wounds of the Lamb as it had been slain.

Oh, precious blood! if better than that of Abel, how much better than all the blood of all the beasts ever slain, than all the sacrifices ever offered, than all the tears or prayers ever presented in the strength of human virtue. We cannot, we will not refuse you, or turn away from your pleading cry, or reject Him who once spoke from the cross, and now speaks from heaven!

CHAPTER 31: THE THINGS THAT CANNOT BE SHAKEN

"This word, 'Yet once more', signifies the removing of those things that are shaken, as of things that are made, that those things which cannot be shaken may remain." (HEBREWS 12.27).

WHAT majesty there is in these words! They bear the mint mark of Deity. No man could presume to utter them, but they become the august Speaker. Their original setting is even more magnificent, as we find them in the Book of Haggai: "Thus says the Lord of hosts. Yet once, it is a little while, and I will shake the heavens, and the earth, and the sea, and the dry land, and I will shake all nations, and the Desire of all nations shall come."

These words were first spoken to encourage the Jewish exiles on their return from Babylon to their ruined Temple and city. The elder men wept as they thought of the departed glories of earlier days, and God comforted them, as He delights to comfort those who are cast down.

"Be comforted," said He in effect, "there is a crisis coming, which will test and overthrow all material structures, and in that convulsion the outer form will pass away, however fair and costly it may be, whilst the inner hidden glory will become more apparent than ever. No, amid all the sounds of wreck and change, there will come the Desire of all nations, the substance of which these material objects are but the fading and incomplete anticipation."

These Hebrew Christians were living in the midst of a great shaking. It was a time of almost universal trial. God was shaking not earth only, but also heaven. The Jewish tenure of Palestine was being shaken by the Romans, who claimed it as their conquest. The interpretation given to the Word of God by the Rabbis was being shaken by the fresh light introduced through the words and life and death of Jesus. The supremacy of the Temple and its ritual was being shaken by those who taught that the true Temple was the Christian Church, and that all the Levitical sacrifices had been realised in Christ. The observance of the Sabbath was being shaken by those who wished to substitute for it the first day of the week.

The first symptoms of this shaking began when Jesus commenced to teach and preach in the crowded cities of Palestine, and all people flocked about him.

The successive throes became more obvious when the Jewish leaders sought to silence the Apostles and stay the onward progress of the Church. The Book of the Acts of the Apostles, and the Epistles, are full of evidence of the intensity of that revolution which must have made many godly people tremble for the Ark of God.

And the climax of all came in the fearful siege of Jerusalem, when, once and forever, the Jewish system was shattered, the Temple burned, the remaining vessels sunk in the Tiber, and the Jews were driven from the city which was absolutely essential for the performance of their religious rites.

The whole New Testament is witness to the throes of one of the mightiest spiritual revolutions that ever happened, as great in the spiritual sphere as the French Revolution was in the temporal.

It was amidst these fires that this Epistle was written. "Take heart," says the inspired writer; "these shakings come from the hand of God." Listen to His own words, 'I shake'. And they shall not last forever, 'yet this once'. Nor will they injure anything of eternal worth and truth. He shakes all things, that the material, the sensuous, and the temporal may pass away; leaving the essential and eternal to stand out in more than former beauty. But not a grain of pure metal shall be lost in the fires, not a fragment of heaven's masonry shall crumble beneath the shock.

In such a time we are living now. Everything is being shaken and tested. But there is a divine purpose in it all, that His eternal truth may stand out more clearly and unmistakably, when all human traditions and accretions have fallen away, unable to resist the energy of the shock. And who will bewail this too bitterly? Who will weep because the winds strip the trees of their old dead leaves, if only the new spring verdure may be able to show itself? Who will lament that the heavy blow shatters the mould, if only the perfect image shall stand out in complete symmetry? Who shall mourn over the passing away of the heaven and the earth, if, as they break up, they reveal beneath them the imperishable beauty of the new heavens and the new earth in which dwells Righteousness?

THEOLOGICAL SYSTEMS ARE BEING SHAKEN. There was a time when men received their theological beliefs from their teachers, their parents, or their Church without a word of question or controversy. There was none that moved the wing, or opened the mouth, or chirped.

It is not so now. The air is filled with questionings. Men are putting into the crucible every doctrine which our forefathers held dear. There is no veneration shown for time honoured creeds or theological distinctions or doctrinal formularies. The highest themes, such as the Nature of the Atonement, the Necessity of Regeneration, the Duration of Future Punishment, are being criticised in the public press.

Many children of God are very distressed about this, and fear for the truth of the Gospel. They speak as if there were no other agents in the conflict but those of mortal birth. They lose sight of the eternal issues at stake, and the unseen forces which are implicated in the conflict.

Is it likely that God will allow His precious Gospel to be overshadowed or robbed of all essential elements? Has He maintained it in its integrity for these ages, and is He now suddenly become a mighty man who cannot save?

When it seemed as if evangelical doctrine had died out of the world in the sixteenth century, because it lingered only amid some obscure and humble saints, He raised up one man, who rolled back the tides of error, and reared once more the standard of Gospel truth, and can He not do it again?

In these terrible shakings, not one jot or tittle of God's Word shall perish, not one grain of truth shall fall to the ground, not one stone in the fortress shall be dislodged. But they are permitted to come, partly to test the chaff and wheat as a winnowing-fan, but chiefly that all which is temporal and transient may pass away, whilst the simple truth of God becomes more apparent, and shines forth unhidden by the scaffolding and rubbish with which the builders have obscured its symmetry and beauty. "The things which cannot be shaken shall remain".

ECCLESIASTICAL SYSTEMS ARE BEING SHAKEN. It is not enough that any religious system should exist; it is asked somewhat rudely to show cause why it should continue to exist. The spirit of the age is utilitarian, and is reluctant to consider any plea for mercy which is not based on a clear evidence of service rendered to its pressing necessities.

The signs of this are abundantly evident. Now it is the Disestablishment of the Church which is proposed, a proposal which fills with horror those who regard it as necessary for the maintenance of Christianity in our midst. Teachers of religion are challenged to show reason for assuming their office, or of claiming special prerogatives. Methods of work are being weighed in the balances, missionary plans trenchantly criticised, religious services metamorphosed.

Change is threatening the most time-honoured customs, and all this is very distressing to those who have confused the essence with the form, the jewel with the casket, the spirit with the temple in which it dwells.

But let us not fear. All this is being permitted for the wisest ends. There is a great deal of wood, hay, and stubble in all our structures which needs to be burned up, but not an ounce of gold or silver will ever be destroyed. The waves may wash off the weed which has attached itself to the harbour wall, but they will fail to start one constituent stone.

The simplicity of early Church life has been undoubtedly covered over with many accretions which hinder the progress of the Church and impede her work, and we may hail any visitation, however drastic, which shall set her free. But the Church herself is founded on a rock, and the gates of Hell shall never prevail against her.

Well was it for the Church of Christ when the days of persecution lay sorely on her. Never was she so pure, so spiritually powerful, as then. And if such days should ever be allowed to return, and God were to shake her fabric with the fierce whirlwinds of martyrdom, there would be no need for anxiety. The time-servers, the mere professors, the creatures of fashion would stand revealed; but those who had experienced the work of God in their souls would endure to the end, and their true character would be manifested. "The things that cannot be shaken will remain."

OUR CHARACTERS AND LIVES ARE CONSTANTLY BEING SHAKEN. What a shake that sermon gave us which showed that all our righteousnesses, on which we counted so fondly, were but withered leaves! What a shake was that commercial disaster which swept away in one blow the savings and credit of years, that were engrossing the heart, and left us only what we had of spiritual worth! What a shake was that temptation which showed that our fancied sinlessness was an empty dream, and that we were as sensitive to temptation as those over whom we had been vaunting ourselves.

What has been the net result of all these shakings? Has a hair of our heads perished? The old man has perished, but the inward man has been daily renewed. The more the marble has wasted, the more the statue has grown. As the wooden centres have been knocked down, the solid masonry has stood out with growing completeness. "The things which could not be shaken have remained."

"Go on, great Spirit of God, shake with Your earthquakes even more violently these characters of ours, that all which is not of You, but of us, and therefore false and selfish, may be revealed and overthrown, so that we may learn our true possessions. And as we see them saved to us from the general wreck, we shall know that, having been given us by Yourself, they must partake of Your own permanence and eternity. Let us learn the worst of ourselves, that we may learn to prize Your best." At the most these shakings are temporary. "Only this once," child of God! Then, nevermore!

THERE ARE A FEW THINGS WHICH CANNOT BE SHAKEN. God's Word. Heaven and earth may pass away, but God's Word never! All flesh is grass, and all the glory of man, his opinions, his pretensions, his pomp and pride, as the flower of grass, beautiful, but evanescent, but the Word of the Lord will stand forever, and this is the Word which by the Gospel is being preached.

Let us not fear modern criticism, it cannot rob us of one jot or tittle of God's truth. Scripture will shake it off, as the Apostle did the viper which fastened on his hand, and felt no hurt.

God's Love. Our friends' love may be shaken by a rumour, a moment's neglect, a change in our estate, but God's love is like Himself, immutable. No storm can reach high enough to touch the empyrean of His love. He never began to love us for anything in ourselves, nor will He cease to love us because of what He discovers us to be. The love of God, which is in Jesus Christ our Lord, is unassailable by change or shock.

God's Eternal Kingdom. "We receive a kingdom which cannot be shaken." Amid all our revolutions and political changes that Kingdom is coming. It is assuming body and shape and power. It is now in mystery, but it shall soon be revealed. And it cannot be touched by any sudden attack or revolt of human passion. "The God of heaven will set up a kingdom, which shall never be destroyed."

Let us count up our inalienable and imperishable treasures, and though around us there is the terror of the darkness or the pestilence of the noontide, we shall be kept in perfect peace, as when some petty sovereign eyes with equanimity the mob arising to sack his palace, because long ago he sent all his treasures to be kept in the strong cellars of the Bank of England.

This world of change and earthquake is not our rest or home. These await us where God lives, in the city which has foundations, and in the land where the storm rages not, but the sea of glass lies peacefully at the foot of the throne of God. We may well brace ourselves to fortitude and patience, to reverence and Godly fear, since we have that in ourselves and yonder which partakes of the nature of God, and neither thieving time can steal it, nor moth corrupt, nor change affect.

It is out of a spirit like this that we are able to offer service that pleases God. Too often there is a self-assumption, a vainglory, an energy of the flesh, that must be in the deepest degree objectionable to His holy, loving eye. It partakes so much of the unrest and chafe of the world around. But when once we breathe the Spirit of the Eternal and Infinite, our hand becomes steadier, our heart quieter, and we learn to receive His grace. We do not agonise for it. We claim and use it, and we serve God with acceptance, through the merits of Jesus Christ our Lord.

CHAPTER 32: GOD A CONSUMING FIRE

"Our God is a consuming fire." (HEBREWS 12.29.)

THIS is one of the shortest texts in the Bible. It takes rank with those other three brief sentences which declare the nature of God, God is Light, God is Love, God is Life. But to many it is one of the most awful sayings in the whole of Scripture.

It rankles in the memory, recurs continually to the uneasy conscience, and rings its wild tocsin of alarm in the ear of the anxious enquirer. And yet there is an aspect in which it may be viewed which will make it one of the most comforting, precious passages in the whole range of inspiration.

Fire is indeed a word significant of horror. To be awakened from sleep by that one awful cry will make the flesh tremble and the heart stand still. A baby's cradle wrapped in flame, a beloved form suddenly enveloped in a burning fiery furnace, a ship on fire amid the wild expanse of the homeless ocean, and slowly burning down to the level of the waves - in any of these figures you have a suggestion of almost unparalleled horror.

And yet, for all that, what comfort and homeliness and genial blessedness there are in the kindly glow of firelight! There is no sign of more abject poverty than the fireless grate. And however warm the rooms may be in Russia or France, the traveller greedily longs for the blaze of the open fireplace of his native land.

Besides, what would we do without this strong, good-natured giant, which toils for us so sturdily? It draws our carriages along the metal track. It drives the machinery of our factories. It disintegrates the precious ore from its rocky matrix. It induces a momentary softness in our toughest metals, so that we can shape them to our will. The arts of civilised life would be impossible but for this Titan worker.

It is obvious, therefore, that whilst Fire is the synonym for horror and dismay, yet it is also full of blessing and goodwill. It is the former only when its necessary laws are violated. It is the latter when those laws are rigorously and reverently observed.

Yes, and are not destruction and ruin the strange and unnatural work of fire, whilst its chosen mission is to bless and beautify and enrich, consuming only the dross and thorns and rubbish, so that there may be a clearer revelation of the enduring realities over which it has no power.

When, therefore, our God is compared to fire, is it only because of the more terrible aspects of His nature, which are to be dreaded by transgressors? Is there not also, and perhaps more largely, a suggestion of those beneficent qualities which are needed for our purity and comfort? Surely there is a strong flavour of such characteristics in the assurance given to us by the prophet Isaiah, "The light of Israel shall be for a fire, and his Holy One for a flame, and it shall burn and devour his thorns and his briers in one day" (Isaiah 10.17).

Fire in the Word of God is not always terrible. When of old God came down on Sinai, its upper peaks were veiled with impenetrable folds of smoke, like the smoke of a furnace. And in the heart of the smoke there was the appearance of devouring fire. There is dread here! Bounds had been set to keep the people back, but a special message must be sent to warn them against breaking through to gaze, lest the fire should break forth upon them.

But there was no harm so long as they kept without the barriers, and when Moses entered into the very heart of it, it did not singe a hair of his head, and injured him no more than when it played round the fragile acacia bush, which burned with fire without being consumed, not a leaf shrivelled, nor a twig scorched.

It is quite true that in the desert pilgrimage there was much of the punitive aspect in the divine fire, as when there came out a fire from the Lord, and consumed the two hundred and fifty men with censers who had joined in Korah's rebellion, and had spoken contemptuously of God's anointed servants. But, on the other hand, it did not hurt one other soul, and these were destroyed, awfully indeed, but almost too suddenly to feel the keen smart of pain. And surely that fire did a beneficent work in staying the further progress of evil, which would have honeycombed the whole nation and led to their destruction as a people.

In the days of Elijah the fire of God consumed two captains and their fifties, but the captains and their troops were full of wanton insolence. There was no hurt done to him who knelt at the mountain foot, beseeching the man of God with reverence and humility. And when, shortly afterward, the great prophet was to go home, it was a chariot of fire in which he sat himself, as in some congenial and friendly element, to waft him to his home.

And on the day of Pentecost when each head bent low beneath the sound as of a mighty rushing wind, a moment afterward each was girt with fire. Apostles, disciples, and women alike experienced this sacred investiture, but it hurt them not. They were far from being perfect characters; and yet there was evidently nothing to fear in the descent of that fiery baptism. They were baptised with the Holy Spirit but they were unconsumed.

Do not these instances shed light upon our text?

OUR GOD IS A CONSUMING FIRE, AND THERE IS TERROR IN THE SYMBOL. But the terror is reserved for those who unceasingly and persistently violate His laws and despise His love. For those who wilfully follow courses of sin, after they have received the knowledge of the truth, there is doubtless a fearful looking for of judgment and fiery indignation. On those who will not obey the Gospel of the Lord Jesus, clearly presented to them, vengeance will be taken in flaming fire.

No words can exaggerate the terror, the anguish, the dreadfulness of their fate. Sin is no light matter. In this world even it is fearfully avenged. Walk through certain wards in our hospitals, and tell me if anything could exceed the horror, the agony, of the penalty which is being inflicted on those who have flagrantly violated the laws of nature.

And, so far as we can see, the physical penalties which follow upon wrongdoing are not unto life and restoration, but unto death and destruction. It is necessary that these sufferings should be veiled from the eye of man, but surely they must be taken into account when we estimate God's treatment of sin. And if such pain, keen as fire, consumes those who violate physical law, surely we must admit that there is a still more awful doom for those who violate the laws of God's love and grace and pleading mercy.

God forbid that we should say one word to lessen men's dread of the penal consequences of sin. There is a great danger lest, amid our growing conceptions of the love of God, we should come to think that He is altogether such a one as we are inclined to be in our dealings with our children, soft, easy, and indulgent.

God is love, and yet He permits the little child to be burned, if it plays heedlessly with flame. God is love, but He permits bodies to rot in loathsome disease, without hope of cure, if men persistently do despite to his law. God is love, but He allows the whole course of a life to be blasted by one yielding to transgression and sin. And thus, though God is love, it is possible for sins to be punished with sufferings, bitter as the gnawing worm, keen as the fire that is not quenched.

If once we realised these things (and we should realise them if we would quietly consider the clear statements of the Word of God on such matters), we would come to understand much better the desperate nature of sin, and to yearn with deeper compassion over those who obstinately resist the grace of God, either following the evil courses suggested by their own hearts, or led captive by the Devil at his will.

O disobedient soul, who has read these words thus far, stop and think of your danger! Beware lest you be as the chaff or thorns, which are burned up with unquenchable fire, on the part of the Lord Himself. Be quick to turn to Him and live. Yet if you suffer irretrievable ruin, remember you will have only yourself to blame, because you have broken the elementary laws of your nature, and have set yourself in opposition to the God who loves you, and would redeem you, but Whom you have refused and defied.

If only you would bend your stubborn neck and submit to shelter yourself in the person and work of Jesus, God's perfect holiness would bring you, not hurt, but blessing and help.

OUR GOD IS A CONSUMING FIRE, AND THERE IS COMFORT AND BLESSING IN THE THOUGHT. When we yield to God's love, and open our hearts to Him, He enters into us, and becomes within us a consuming fire, not to ourselves, but to the evil within us. So that, in a very deep and blessed sense, we may be said to dwell with the devouring fire, and to walk amid the eternal burnings.

Fire is warmth. We talk of ardent desire, warm emotion, enthusiasm's glow and fire; and when we speak of God being within us as fire, we mean that He will produce in us a strong and constant affection to Himself. Do you long for more love? You really need more of God, for God is love, and when He dwells in the heart, love dwells there in power. And there is no difficulty in loving Him or loving men with the love which has entered in majestic procession in the entrance of God.

Live in God, make room for God to live in you, and there will be no lack to the love which shall exemplify in daily action each precept of the holy psalm of love (1 Corinthians 13).

Fire is light. We are dark enough in our natural state, but when God comes into the tabernacle of our being, the shekinah begins to glow in the most holy place, and pours its waves of glory throughout the whole being, so that the face is suffused with a holy glow, and there is an evident elasticity and buoyancy of spirits which no world joy can produce or even imitate.

The light that shone on the face of Moses was different from that which shone on the face of Jesus. That was flung on it from without; this welled up from within. But the latter rather than the former is the true type of the blessed effect produced on that nature which becomes the temple of the indwelling God.

Fire is purity. How long, think you, would it take a workman with hammer and chisel to get the ore from the rocks in which it lies so closely imbedded? But if they are flung into the great cylinder, and the fires fanned to torrid heat, and the draught roars through the burning mass, at nightfall the glowing stream of pure and fluid metal, from which all dross and rubbish are parted, flows into the waiting mould. This is a parable of what God will do for us. No, more, He will burn up the wood, hay, and stubble, the grit and dross, the selfishness and evil of our nature, so that at last only the gold and silver and precious stones will remain. The bonds that fetter us will be consumed, but not a hair of our heads will fall to the ground.

"The Lord shall sit as a refiner of silver." He the refiner, and He the fire. Contact with God, being bathed in His Holy Spirit, the perpetual yielding of the nature to Him, will work a marvellous change on us. At first the face of the melting metal may be dark and lurid - deep orange red, over which a flickering flame will pass, but, as the process is pursued, the colour will become lighter, the dark fumes will pass off, and the metal shall bear the appearance of the highly polished mirror, reflecting the beholder's face. The process may be long, but the result is sure.

Is not fire painful and terrible, though applied by infinite love? It may be so, but He will not ply us with more than we can bear, and He will enable us to endure. And it will be more than a compensation, as we find one after another of the old evils losing its power.

We will never in this life be free from a sinful tendency, which seems part of our human nature. Nor will we ever, on this side of heaven, be perfect, but we may expect to be growingly transformed into the image of the Son of God.

0h God, Who is as fire, be a consuming fire to our inbred sins, burn deeply into our inmost hearts, until all that grieves You is compelled to yield to the holy intensity of Your grace, and our whole being, made free from sin, begins to serve You in holiness and righteousness, through Jesus Christ, who came to kindle Your Sacred Fire on the earth!

CHAPTER 33: THE UNCHANGING SAVIOUR

"Jesus Christ, the same yesterday, and today, and forever." (HEBREWS 13.8).

THREE times over in this chapter, the closing chapter of an Epistle the study of which has been so pleasant and helpful, the sacred writer urges his readers to think kindly of those who ruled over them. The full force of the Greek word is better represented by the marginal rendering guide, than by the word rule. But in any case he referred to those who were the spiritual leaders and teachers of the flock.

The three injunctions are - Remember (verse 7); Obey (verse 7); Salute (verse 23).

It is a proud name for the Christian minister to be called a leader. But unless he has some other claim to it than comes from force of character, eloquence, or intellectual power, his name will be an empty sound, the sign of what he might be rather than of what he is. Those who are qualified to lead other men must be themselves close followers of Christ, so that they may be able to turn to others and say, "Be you followers of me, even as I also am of Christ." "Be followers together with Me."

But the Christian minister must also watch for souls (verse 17). He is not sent to his charge to preach great sermons, to elaborate brilliant orations, or to dazzle their intellects, but to watch over their souls, as the shepherd watches over his flocks scattered on the downs, while the light changes from the grey morning, through the deep tints of the noon, into the last delicate flush of evening far up on the loftiest cliffs. He must indeed keep careful watch, for he must give an account in the evening, of his hand every missing one will be required.

It is told of the holy Melville, that his wife would sometimes find him on his knees in the cold winter night, and on asking him to return to bed, he would reply, "I have got fifteen hundred souls in my charge, and fear that it is going ill with some of them." It is not difficult to remember or obey or salute men like that. They carry their Master's sign upon their faces. They are among Christ's most precious gifts to His Church.

But there is this sorrow connected with all human leaders and teachers. However dear and useful they are, they are not suffered to continue by reason of death. One after another they pass away into the spirit world, to enter upon their loftier service, to give in their account, to see the Master whom they have loved. The last sermon lies unfinished on the study table, but they never come there to complete it. The final word is spoken. The closing benediction is given. The ministry is done.

But what a relief it is to turn from men to Christ, from the constant change in human teachers to the unchanging Master, from the under-shepherds who are here today but gone tomorrow, to the chief Shepherd and Bishop of souls who watches His sheep in the evening shadows of this era, equally as in the first bright beams of its Pentecostal morning!

This is the meaning of our writer (verse 7). The verb is in the past tense: "Remember them which had the rule over you, such as spoke to you the word of God, the end of whose life considering, imitate their faith." Evidently they had been lately called to witness the end of the life and ministry of some who had been very precious to them. And, as their hearts were sorrowing, their attention was turned from the changing guide and leader to the ever-living, unchanging Lord, Jesus Christ, who is the same yesterday, today, and forever.

WHAT IS DENIED. It is denied that either time or mood or circumstances or provocation or death can alter Jesus Christ our Lord.

Time changes us. Your portrait, taken years ago, when you were in your prime, hangs on the walls of your home. You sometimes sadly contrast it with your present self. Then the eye flashed with fires which have been quenched with many tears. Then the hair was raven and thick, which is now plentifully streaked with the grey symptoms of decay. Then the face was unseamed by care, unscarred by conflict, but now how weary and furrowed! The upright form is bent, the step has lost its spring.

But there is a greater difference between two mental and two physical portraitures. Opinions alter. The radical becomes conservative, temper changes, and affections cool. Names and faces which used to thrill are recalled without emotion. Faded chaplets lie where once flowers of rarest texture yielded their breath in insufficient adoration. Thus is it with those who are born of woman. Time does for them what hardship and authority and suffering would fail to effect.

And sometimes the question arises, 'can time alter Him whose portrait hangs on the walls of our hearts, painted in undying colours by the hands of the four Evangelists?

Of course, time takes no effect on God, who is the I AM, eternal and changeless. But Jesus is man as well as God. He has tenses in His being, the yesterday of the past, the today of the present, the tomorrow of the future. It is at least a question whether His human nature, keyed to the experiences of man, may not carry with it, even to influence His royal heart, that sensitiveness to the touch of time which is characteristic of our race.

But the question tarries only for a second. The moment it utters itself it is drowned by the great outburst of voices which exclaim, "He is the same in the meridian day of the present as He was in the yesterday of his earthly life, and He will be the same when tomorrow we shall have left far behind us the shores of time and are voyaging with Him over the tideless, stormless depths of the ocean of eternity."

If we could ask the blessed dead if they had found Him altered from what they had expected Him to be from the pages of the holy Gospels, they would reiterate the words of the angels - this same Jesus. They would tell us that His hair is white as snow, not with age, but with the light of intense purity, that His face shines still as the sun in his strength, with no sign of westering, and that His voice is as full as when He summoned Lazarus from the grave, as sweet as when it called Mary to recognise him. Time is foiled in Jesus. He has passed out of its sphere, and is impervious to its spell.

Moods change us. We know people who are like oranges one day and lemons the next, now a summer's day, and, again, a nipping frost, rock and reed alternately. You have to suit yourself to their varying mood, asking today what you would not dare to mention tomorrow, and thus there is continual unrest and scheming in the hearts of their friends.

But it is not so with Jesus. Never tired, or put out, or variable. Without shadow cast by turning. In His earthly life, wherever we catch sight of him - on the mountainside, on the waters of the lake, beneath the olive trees in the evening, in the synagogue, or alone, at work in the sunlight, at prayer in the moonlight, at supper in the upper room, He was always the same Jesus.

And the apparent exceptions when, for a certain purpose, He altered His manner and made Himself strange, only brought His essential sameness into stronger relief. And so is He today. And we shall become happy and strong when we remove from all thought of others' moods or our own, and settle down under the unchanging empyrean of His love.

Circumstances change us. Men who in poverty and obscurity have been accessible and genial, become imperious and haughty when they become idolised for their genius and fawned on for their wealth. The butler who would have done any favour for Joseph in the prison forgot him when he was reinstated in the palace. New friends, new spheres, new surroundings, alter men marvellously.

What a change has passed over Jesus Christ since mortal eyes beheld Him! Crowned with glory and honour, seated at the right hand of the Father; occupied with the government of all worlds, worshipped by the loftiest spirits. Can this be He who trod our world, confessing His ignorance of times and seasons, surrounded by a handful of the poor and despised, an outcast and a sufferer? It is indeed He.

But surely it were too much to expect that He should be quite the same! No, but He is. And one proof of it is that the graces which He shed on the first age of the Church were of exactly the same quality as those which we now enjoy.

We know that the texture of light is unaltered, because the analysis of a ray, which has just reached us from some distant star, whence it started as Adam stepped across the threshold of Eden, is of precisely the same nature as the analysis of the ray of light now striking on this page. And we know that Jesus Christ is the same as He was, because the life which throbbed in the first believers resulted in those very fruits which are evident in our own hearts and lives, all having emanated from Himself.

He has to govern the worlds, but He is still as accessible to the vilest, as gentle and tender-hearted, as humble and lovely, as when that Jewish woman could not restrain her envy of the mother who had borne Him, and when He sat to rest amid the sycamores of Bethany, and the sisters rested by His feet.

Sin and provocation change us. We forgive seven times, but draw the line at eight. Our souls close up to those who have deceived our confidence. We are friendly outwardly, but there is frost within. We forgive, but we do not forget, and we are never the same afterward as before.

But sin cannot change Christ's heart, though it may affect His behaviour. If it could do so, it must have changed His feelings to Peter. But the only apparent alteration made by that sad denial was an increased tenderness and considerateness. "Go, tell my disciples, and Peter, that I am risen."

"He was seen of Cephas, then of the twelve." "He said unto Peter, Do you love me?"

Your sins may be many and aggravated, and you are disposed to think that you should give up all profession of being His at all. But you do not know Him. He is not oblivious to your sins. He has noticed each one with sharp pangs of pain. His eye has followed you in all your way ward wanderings. But He is absolutely unchanged. You are as dear to Him as when, in the first blush of your young hope, you knelt at His feet, and were clothed, as the old warriors used to be, by a stainless tunic over your armour of proof.

Naught that you have said or done has lessened His love by a single grain, or turned it aside by a hair's-breadth. He loved you in eternity. He foreknew all that you would be before He set His heart upon you. He cannot be surprised by any sudden outburst of your evil. You may be, but He cannot be, and He laid His account for this, and more, when He undertook to redeem. Your sins, 0h child of God, can no more alter your Lord's heart than can the petulance of a child alter its mother's.

WHAT IS AFFIRMED. He is the same in His Person (Hebrews 1.12). His vesture alters. He has exchanged the gaberdine of the peasant for the robes of which He stripped Himself on the eve of His incarnation, but beneath those robes beats the same heart as heaved with anguish at the grave where His friend lay dead. We shall yet see, though in resurrection glory, the face on which stood the bead-drops of bloody sweat, and touch the hands that were nailed to the cross, and hear the voice of the Son of man.

What does the mystery of the forty days teach us, except this, that He carried with Him from the grave, and upward to His home, the identical body of his incarnation - though the corruptible had put on incorruption, and the mortal had put on immortality? Thus He is the same "Jesus."

He is also the same in his Priesthood (Hebrews 7.24). Aaron died on Hor, and all his successors in mystic procession followed him. Ancient burying-grounds are closely packed with the remains of priests, abbots, and fathers. The ashes of the shepherds are mingled with those of their flocks. The office remains, but the occupants pass.

But Christ, as the Anointed Priest, is ever the same. Unweariedly He pursues His chosen work as the Mediator, Priest, and Intercessor of men. He does not fail, nor is He discouraged. Though the great world of men neither knows nor heeds Him, yet does He bear it up on His heart, as when He first pleaded for His murderers from His cross. "Forgive them, Father, forgive them !" is His unwearying constant cry. And though the age be black with tempest and red with blood, His pity wells up like one of those perennial fountains which heat cannot scorch, nor cold freeze, because they draw their supplies from everlasting sources. He is the same "Christ."

WHAT IT IMPLIES. It implies that He is God. It implies, too, that the Gospels are a leaf out of His eternal diary, and may be taken as a true record of His present life. What He was, He is. He still sails with us in the boat; walks in the afternoon with us to Emmaus, stands in our midst at nightfall, opening to us the Scriptures. He wakes our children in the morning with His "Talitha cumi", calls the boys to His knees, watches them at their play, and rebukes those who would forbid their Hosannas.

He feeds us with bread and fish, lights fires on the sands to warm us, shows us the right side of the ship for our nets, and interests Himself with the results of our toils. He takes us with Him to the brow of the Transfiguration Mount, and into the glades of Gethsemane.

When we are slow to believe, He is slower still to anger. He teaches us many things, graduating His lessons, according to our ability to understand. When we cannot bear more, He shades the light. When we strive for high places, He rebukes. When soiled, He washes our feet. When in peril, He comes across the yeasty waves to our help. When weary, He leads us aside to rest.

Oh, do not read the Gospels as a record merely of the past, but as a transcript of what He is ever doing. Each miracle and parable and trait is a specimen of eternal facts, which are taking place by myriads, at every moment of the day and night; the achievements of the ever-living, ever-working Lord. No lake without that figure treading its waters. No storm without that voice mightier than its roar. No meal without that face uplifted in blessing, or that hand engaged in breaking. No grave without that tender heart touched with sorrow. No burden without those willing shoulders to share the yoke.

Oh, take me not back through the long ages to a Christ that was! He is! He lives! He is here! I can never again be alone, never grope in the dark for a hand, never be forsaken or forlorn. Never need a Guide, a Master, a Friend, or a Husband to my soul. I have Him, who suffices for uncounted myriads in the dateless noon of eternity.

He who was everything in the yesterday of the past, and who will be everything in the tomorrow of the future, is mine today; and at each present moment of my existence - here, and in all worlds.

The Revised Version adds a significant 'yes' to this verse, to bring out the emphatic accentuation which the writer lays upon the unchangeableness of Jesus. It is well placed. And with what a thunder of assent might that word be uttered! All who are of this opinion answer YES. First, the innumerable company of angels utters it, then the spirits of just men made perfect reaffirm it, then the universe of created things, the regularity of whose laws and processes is due to it, bursts forth with one great Amen. God himself says Amen, "for how many soever be the promises of God, in Him is the yes, wherefore also through Him is the Amen, to the glory of God.

CHAPTER 34: THE ESTABLISHED HEART

"It is a good thing that the heart be established with grace, not with meats, which have not profited those who have been occupied therein." (HEBREWS 13.9.

IT is a good thing to have an established heart. With too many of us the inner life is variable and fickle. Sometimes we have days of deep religious earnestness, when it seems impossible for us to spend too long a time in prayer and fellowship with God. The air is so clear that we can see across the waters of the dividing sea, to the very outlines of the heavenly coasts. But a very little will mar our peace, and bring a veil of mist over our souls, to enwrap us perhaps for long weeks. Oh for an established heart!

Now there is one thing which will not bring about this blessed state of establishment. And that is indicated by the expression, "meats", which stands for the ritualism of the Jewish law. There is ever a tendency in the human heart toward a religion of rites. It is so much easier to observe the prescriptions of an outward ceremonial than to brace the soul to faith and love and spiritual worship.

Set the devotee a round of external observance, it matters little how rigorous and searching your demands, and the whole will be punctually and slavishly performed, with a secret sense of satisfaction in being thus permitted to do something toward procuring acceptance and favour with God.

There is a great increase of ritualistic observance amongst us. We behold with astonishment the set of our times toward genuflexions, the austerities of Lent, the careful observance of prolonged and incessant services, and all the demands of a severe ritual. People who give no evidence in their character or behaviour of real religion are most punctilious in these outward religious rites. Young men will salve their consciences for a day of Sabbath-breaking by an early celebration.

In many cases these things are revivals of ancient Babylonish customs, passed into the professing Church in the worst and darkest days of its history. But their revival points to the strong religious yearnings of human nature, and the fascination which is exerted by outward rites in the stead of inward realities.

But "meats" can never establish the inner life. The most ardent ritualist must confess to the sense of inward dissatisfaction and unrest, as the soul is condemned to pace continually the arid desert of a weary formalism, where it comes not to the green pastures or the waters of rest. "They have not profited them those who have been occupied therein."

Another obstruction to an established heart arises from the curiosity which is ever running after divers and strange doctrines. In all ages of the Church men have caught up single aspects of truth, distorting them out of the harmony of the Gospel, and carrying them into exaggerated and dangerous excess, and directly any one truth is viewed out of its place in the equilibrium of the Gospel, it becomes a heresy, leading souls astray with the deceitfulness of the false lights that wreckers wave along the beach.

And when once we begin to follow the vagaries and notions of human teachers, apart from the teaching of the Spirit of God, we get into an unsettled, restless condition, which is the very antipodes to the established heart.

There is only one foundation which never rocks, one condition which never alters. "It is good that the heart be established with grace." Primarily, of course, the established heart is the gift of God. "He which stablishes us with you in Christ is God." "The Lord shall establish you an holy people unto Himself." "The God of all grace make you perfect, stablish, strengthen, settle you." We need therefore to pray to Him to give us the heart established in grace.

But there are certain conditions also indicated in this context with which we do well to comply.

WE MUST FEED ON CHRIST. The very denial of the tenth verse proves that there is an altar whereof we have a right to eat. Not the Jews only, but Christians also, lay stress on eating; but ah, how different the food which forms their diet ! In the case of that ancient system out of which these Hebrew Christians had just emerged, the priests ate a considerable portion of the sacrifices which the people offered on the altar of God. This was the means of their subsistence.

In consideration of their being set apart wholly to the divine service, and having no inheritance in the land, "they lived by the altar." But we, who are priests by a finer right, have left behind us the Tabernacle, with its ritual and sacrifices, and cannot feed on these outward meats without betraying the spirituality of the holy religion we profess.

Our altar is the cross. Our sacrifice is the dying Saviour. Our food is to eat His flesh. "This is the bread which comes down from heaven, that a man may eat thereof, and not die." "The bread is My flesh, which I will give for the life of the world."

Eating consists of three processes, apprehension, mastication, and assimilation, and each of these has its spiritual counterpart in that feeding upon Christ which is the very life of our life. We, too, must apprehend Him, by the careful reading of the Word of God. The Word is in the words. His words are spirit and life.

We need not be always reading them, any more than we should be always eating. But just as a good meal will go on nourishing us long after we have taken it, and indeed when we have ceased to think about it, so a prolonged prayerful study of the Word of God will nourish our souls for long afterward.

meditating long and thoughtfully on all that is revealed to us in the Word of the person and work of the Lord Jesus. It is only by allowing our heart and mind to dwell musingly on these sacred themes that they become so real as to nourish us. Better read less and meditate more, than read much and meditate little.

We too must assimilate Christ, until He becomes part of our very being, and we begin to live, yet not we, because Christ lives in us, and has become our very life. Our Lord told His disciples that He lived by the Father; and said that, if they desired to live in the same dependent state on Himself, they must "eat him " (John 6.57).

In Christ's own case His being had reached such a pitch of union with His Father's that to see or hear or know Him was to see and hear and know God. And if we would only spend more time alone with Him in prayerful, loving fellowship, a great change would pass over us also, and we will be transformed into His likeness in successive stages of glory upon glory.

At regular intervals we meet around the table of the Lord to eat the bread and drink the wine. But our feeding on Him ought to be as frequent as our daily ordinary meals.

Why should we feed the spirit less than we do the body? Alas! how we pamper the latter, and starve the former, until we get past the sense of desire! We spoil our appetite by feeding it with the cloying sweetmeats and morsels of sense. We are content to live as parasites on the juices of others, instead of acquiring nourishment at first hand for ourselves.

What wonder that we are carried about by every wind of doctrine, and lack the established heart? And perhaps there would be nothing better for the whole of us Christian people than a revival of Bible study, a fresh consecration of the morning hour, a regular and systematic maintenance of seasons of prolonged fellowship with our Master and Lord.

IF WE WOULD FEED ON CHRIST, WE MUST GO WITHOUT THE CAMP. In the solemn ritual of the great Day of Atonement it was ordained that the bodies of all the victims which had suffered death as sin-offerings, and of which the blood had been sprinkled before the mercy-seat, should be burned Without the camp (Leviticus 16.27). And in this mysterious specification, two truths were probably symbolised. First, that in the fullness of time, Jesus, the true sin-offering of the world, would suffer outside the city gate, and secondly, that men must leave the principles and rites of earthly systems behind them, if they would realise all the blessedness of acceptance with God through the sacrifice of Christ.

If, then, we would have Jesus as our food, our joy, our life, we must not expect to find Him in the camps which have been pitched by men of this world. We must go forth from all such, from the camp of the world's religiousness equally as from that of its sensuality; from the tents of its formalism and ritualism, as well as from those of its vanity.

The policy of going forth without the camp is the only safe course for ourselves, as it is the only helpful one for the world itself. There are plenty who argue that the wisest policy is to stop within the camp, seeking to elevate its morals. They do not realise that, if we adopt their advice, we must remain there alone, for our Lord has already gone.

It is surely unbefitting that we should find a home where He is expelled. What is there in us which makes us so welcome, when our Master was cast out to the fate of the lowest criminals? Besides, it will not be long before we discover that, instead of our influencing the camp for good, the atmosphere of the camp will infect us with its evil. Instead of our levelling it up, it will level us down.

The only principle of moving the world is to emulate Archimedes in getting to a point without it. All the men who have left a mark in the elevation of their times have been compelled to join the pilgrim host which is constantly passing through the city gates, and taking up its stand by the cross on which Jesus died. Looking back on that memorable spot, we seem to see it thronged with the apostles, martyrs, reformers, and prophets of every age, who invite us to join them. It remains with us to say whether we will linger amid the luxury and fascinations which allure us to the camp, or whether we will dare to take up our cross, and follow our Master along the Way of Sorrow, bearing His reproach.

Ah, young hearts, secret disciples, halters between two opinions, the issue of such a choice cannot be doubtful! With the cry, 'God wills it' you will join this new crusade, and take your stand with Jesus, at the trysting-place of His cross.

IF WE GO OUTSIDE THE CAMP, WE MUST BEAR HIS REPROACH. It is related of the good Charles Simeon, of Cambridge, that, at the commencement of his career as an evangelical clergyman at Cambridge, he encountered such virulent abuse and opposition that his spirit seemed on the point of being crushed. Turning to the Word of God for direction and encouragement, his eye lighted on the following passage: " As they came out they found a man of Cyrene, Simon by name. Him they compelled to bear His cross."

The similarity of the name to his own arrested him, and he was moved to new courage with the thought of his oneness with the sufferings of Jesus. So is it with us all. If we are reproached for the name of Jesus, happy are we, and we should rejoice, inasmuch as we are partakers of Christ's sufferings, that, when His glory is revealed, we also may be glad with exceeding joy.

How marvellous is it to learn the closeness of the bonds by which we are bound to the saints of the past When we are reproached for being Christians, we know something of what Moses felt when taunted in the royal palace of Egypt with his Hebrew origin, but "he esteemed the reproach of Christ greater riches than all the treasures of Egypt, because he had respect unto the recompense of reward."

BUT WHILST BEARING CHRIST'S REPROACH, WE SHALL FIND THE ONLY CONTINUING CITY. It is very remarkable that, as we tear ourselves away from the gate of the city, and say farewell to what had seemed to be a symbol of the most enduring fabrics of earthly permanence, we are really passing out of the transient and unreal to become citizens of the only enduring and continuing City.

The greatest cities of human greatness have not continued. Babylon, Nineveh, Thebes, the mighty cities of Mexico - all have passed. Buried in mounds, on which grass grows luxuriantly; while wild beasts creep through the mouldering relics of the past. But, amid all, there is arising from age to age a permanent structure, an enduring City, a confederation which gathers around the unchanging Saviour, and has in it no elements of decay.

Do we enough live in this City in our habitual experience? It is possible to tread its golden streets as we plod along the thoroughfares of earth's great cities, to mingle in its blessed companies, and share its holy exercises, though apparently we spend our days in dark city offices, and amid money-loving companions. The true pilgrim to the City really lives in the City. It will not be long, and it shall not be only an object for faith and spiritual vision, it shall become manifest.

See, it comes! it comes! the holy City out of heaven from God, radiant with his light, vocal with song, the home of saints, the metropolis of a redeemed earth, the Bride of the Lamb, for whom the universe was made.

CHAPTER 35: THE CLOSING PRAYER

"Now the God of peace, that brought again from the dead our Lord Jesus, that great Shepherd of the sheep, through the blood of the everlasting covenant, make you perfect in every good work to do His will, working in you that which is well pleasing in His sight, through Jesus Christ, to Whom be glory for ever and ever. HEBREWS 13.20, 21).

THROUGHOUT this Epistle, the inspired writer has been appealing to man. Through successive paragraphs he has poured forth a burning stream of argument, remonstrance, or appeal, now opening the full peal of Sinai's thunders, and now the wail of Calvary's broken heart, and finally summoning the most honoured names in Hebrew story to enforce his words.

All this is over now. He can say no more. The ploughing and sowing and harrowing are alike complete. He must turn from earth to heaven, from man to God, and leave his converts and his work with that glorious Being whose cause he had striven so faithfully to plead, and who alone could crown his labours with success.

There are many splendid outbursts of prayer beginning these Epistles, but amongst them all, it is impossible to find one more striking or beautiful than this.

THE BURDEN OF THE PRAYER is that these Hebrew Christians may be made perfect to do God's will. The word "perfect" means to set in joint, or articulate. Naturally, we are out of joint, or, at the best, work stiffly, but the ideal of Christian living is to be so perfectly "set" that God's purposes may be easily and completely realised in us.

There is no higher aim in life than to do the will of God. It was the supreme object for which our Saviour lived. This brought Him from heaven. This determined His every action. This fed His inner life with hidden meat. This cleared and lit up His judgment. This led Him with unfaltering decision into the valley of death. This was the stay and solace of His spirit as he drank the bitter cup of agony.

Throughout His mortal life His one glad shout of assurance and victory was, "I delight to do Your will, Oh my God. Yes, Your law is within my heart." And human lives climb up from the lowlands to the upland heights just in proportion as they do the will of God on earth as it is done in heaven. If every reader of these lines would resolve from this moment to do the will of God in the very smallest things - with scrupulous care, counting nothing insignificant, shrinking from no sacrifice, evading no command - life would assume entirely a new aspect. There might be a momentary experience of suffering and pain, but it would be succeeded by the light of resurrection, and the new song of heaven, stealing like morning through the chambers of the soul.

God is love. To do His will is to scatter love in handfuls of blessing on a weary world.
God is light. To do His will is to tread a path that shines more and more unto the perfect day.
God is life. To do His will is to eat of the Tree of Life, and live forever, and to drink deep draughts of the more abundant life which Jesus gives.
God is the God of hope. To do His will is to be full of all joy and peace, and to abound in hope.
God is the God of all comfort. To do His will is to be comforted in all our tribulation by the tender love of a mother.
God is the God of peace. To do His will is to learn the secret inner calm, which no storm can reach, no tempest ruffle.
God is the God of truth. To do His will is to be on the winning side, and to be assured of the time when He will bring out our righteousness as the light, and our judgment as the noonday.

Why will you not, my readers, who have followed these chapters thus far to the last, resolve from this moment that your will shall henceforth say "Yes" to God's will, and that you will live out what He wills and works within? Probably, at the very outset, you will be tested by your attitude to some one thing. Do not try to answer all the suggestions or enquiries that may be raised tumultuously within, but deal immediately and decisively with that single item. Dare to say, with respect to it, "I will Your will, Oh my God." And immediately the gate will open into the rapture of a new life.

But remember that His will must be done in every work to which you put your hands, and thenevery work will be good.

We cannot tell how the mysterious promptings of our will are able to express themselves in our limbs and members. We only know that what we will in ourselves is instantly wrought out through the wonderful machinery of nerve and muscle. And we are quick to perceive when, through some injury or dislocation, the mandate of the will fails to be instantly and completely fulfilled. Nor do we rest content until the complete communication is restored.

But in all this there is a deep spiritual analogy. We are members, through grace, of the body of Christ. The will lies with Him, and if we were living as we ought, we should be incessantly conscious of its holy impulses, withdrawing us from this, or prompting us to that. Our will would not be obliterated, but would elect to work in perpetual obedience and subordination to the will of its King.

Alas! this is not our case. We are too little sensible of those holy impulses. On rare occasions we realise and yield to them. But how many of them fail to reach or move us, because we are out of joint! What prayer could better befit our lips than that the God of peace, the true surgeon of souls, would put us in joint, to do His will, with unerring accuracy, promptitude, and completeness!

MARK THE GUARANTEES THAT THIS PRAYER SHALL BE REALISED. The appeal is made to the God of peace. He Whose nature is never swept by the storms of desire or unrest, Whose one aim is to introduce peace into the heart and life, Whose love to us will not brook disappointment in achieving our highest blessedness, He must undertake this office. He will do it most tenderly and delicately, nor will He rest until the obstruction to the inflow of His nature is removed, and there is perfect harmony between the promptings of His will and our immediate and joyous response.

He brought again from the dead our Lord Jesus, that great Shepherd of the sheep. To have given us a Shepherd was much, but to have given us so great a Shepherd is marvellous. He is the great Shepherd Who died, just as He is the good Shepherd Who knows His flock, and the chief Shepherd Who is coming again. He is great, because of the intrinsic dignity of His nature, because of His personal qualifications to save and bless us, because of the greatness of His unknown sufferings; and because of the height of glory to which the Father has exalted Him.

The words "brought again" are very expressive. They contain the idea of "brought up." More is meant than the reanimation of the dead body of Christ. There is included, also, His exaltation by the right hand of God, to be a Prince and a Saviour. And, surely, if our God has given us such a Shepherd, and raised Him to such a glory, that He may help us the more efficiently, there is every reason why we should confidently count on His doing all that may needed in us, as He has done all that was needed for us.

He will certainly respect the everlasting covenant, which has been sealed with blood. God has entered into an eternal covenant with us to be our God and Friend. That covenant, which does not depend on anything in us, but rests on His own unchanging nature, has been ratified by the precious blood of His Son.

As the first covenant was sealed by the sprinkled blood of slain beasts, so the second was sealed by the precious blood of Christ. "This is My blood of the new testament, which is shed for many for the remission of sins." Thus spoke our Saviour on the eve of His death, with a weight of meaning which this Epistle was needed to explain.

And is it likely that He who has entered into such a covenant with our souls - a covenant so everlasting, so divine, so solemn - will ever go back from it, or allow anything to remain undone which may be needed to secure its perfect and efficient operation? It cannot be! We may count, without the slightest hesitation, on the God of peace doing all that is required to perfect us in every good work to do His will.

THE DIVINE METHOD will be to 'work in us'. It is necessary first that we should be adjusted so that there may be no waste or diversion of the divine energy. When that is done, then it will begin to pass into and through us in mighty tides of power.

"God working in you." It is a marvellous expression! We know how steam works mightily within the cylinder, forcing the ponderous piston up and down. We know how sap works mightily within the branches, forcing itself out in bud and leaf and blossom. We read of a time when men and women were so possessed of devils that they spoke and acted as the inward promptings led them. These are approximations to the conception of the text, which towers infinitely beyond.

Have we not all been conscious of some of these workings? They do not work in us mightily as they did in the Apostle Paul, because we have not yielded to them as he did. Still, we have known them when the breath of holy resolution has swept through our natures, or we have conceived some noble purpose, or have been impelled to some deed of self-sacrifice for others.

These are the workings of God within the heart, not in the tornado only, but in the zephyr, not in the thunder alone, but in the still small voice. Every sigh for the better life, every strong and earnest resolution, every determination to leave the nets and fishing-boats to follow Jesus, every appetite for fellowship, every aspiration heavenward - all these are the result of God's in-working.

How careful we should be to gather up every divine impulse, and translate it into action! We must work out what He works in. We must labour according to His working, which works in us mightily. We must be swift to seize the fugitive and transient expression, embodying it in the permanent act.

It does not seem so difficult to live and work for God when it is realised that the eternal God is energising within. You cannot be sufficiently patient to that querulous invalid, your patience is exhausted, but God is working His patience within you. Let it come out through you. You cannot muster strength for that obvious Christian duty, but God is working that fruit in your innermost nature. Be content to let it manifest itself by you. You are incompetent to sustain that Christian work, with its manifold demands, but stand aside, and let the eternal God work in and through you, to do by His strength what you in your weakness cannot do.

The Christian is the workshop of God. In that mortal but renewed nature the divine Artisan is at work, elaborating products of exquisite beauty and marvellous skill. Would that we might be less eager to give the world ourselves, and more determined that there should be a manifestation through all the gateways of our being of the wondrous in-working of the God of peace! Then we might say, with some approach to the words of our Lord, to such as demand evidences of His resurrection and life, "How do you say, prove to me the resurrection of Jesus? The words which I speak, I speak not of myself, but my Saviour, who dwells in me, He does the works."

THE RESULT will be that we shall be well-pleasing in His sight, through Jesus Christ. Our good works can never be the ground of our acceptance or justification. The very best of them can only please God through Jesus Christ. Our purest tears need washing again in His blood. Our holiest actions need to be cleansed ere they can be viewed by a holy God. Our best prayers and gifts need to be laid on the altar which sanctifies all it touches. We could not stand before God for a moment, save by that one sufficient substitutionary sacrifice, once offered by Jesus on the cross, and now pleaded by Him before the throne.

At the same time, our Father is pleased with our obedient loyalty to His will. He gives us this testimony, that we please Him, as Enoch did, who walked with Him before the flood. And it should be the constant ambition of our lives so to walk as to please Him, and to obtain from Him a faint echo of those memorable words which greeted our Saviour as He stepped into the waters of Baptism, "This is my beloved Son, in whom I am well pleased."

To Him be glory for ever and ever! Directly the soul is right with God, it becomes a vehicle for God, and thus a revenue of glory begins to accrue to God, which ceases not, but augments as the years roll by. And the time will never come when the spirit shall not still pour forth its glad rejoicings to the glory of Him to Whom is due the praise of all.

If your life is not bringing glory to God, see to it that at once you set to work to ascertain the cause. Learning it, let it be dealt with forthwith. Hand yourself over to God to make you and keep you right. And thus begin a song of love and praise, which shall rise through all coming ages, to the Father who chose you in Christ, to the Saviour who bought you with His blood, and to the Spirit who sanctifies the heart, one adorable Trinity, to Whom be the glory for ever and ever, Amen.